7 RULES

TO A

GOOD

LIFE

THE TIME TO LEARN IS NOW!

DAVE ARMSTRONG

Permissions:
New Song by Howard Jones (released August
1983) permission given 26 January 2023

An audio-visual package supports this book available on: Live
Life Smarter YouTube Channel (subscription required)
https://www.youtube.com/@
livelifesmartercoachingpro6615/featured

ISBN: 978-1-3999-6979-6

Edited by C J Harter www.cjharterbooks.co.uk
Cover and interior design by Victoria Wolf,
wolfdesignandmarketing.com

Available on Audible
Audible version recorded by Greg Veryard at 80Hrz Studio
Audible narrated by Jed Simpson

Harback and paperback editions of this book are available.

This book is dedicated to:

Brian (Budgie) Marsden
Paul Metcalfe
An unknown Argentinian soldier
Nicky Armstrong

whose stories inspired me to write this book.

Special mention to my partner Anna and her son Matthew

CONTENTS

INTRODUCTION

THERE ARE TWO CERTAINTIES IN LIFE: you are born and you die. The uncertainty in life is found in the bit between. The unknown in life is when it will end. If we are honest with ourselves, we all want to live a good life. The good news is the good life is here if you want it.

So, what does the complete good life look like?

It can be as simple as quality time with family or friends and seeing your children and grandchildren grow up; or it could mean fulfilling a dream of seeing people back on the moon, curing cancer or becoming rich and powerful. Whatever your vision of a good life may be, its origin is within your mind and soul.

The big question is: are you living the good life now? If not, when and how can you make it happen? The German philosopher Friedrich Nietzsche[1] talked about how you can be the agent, the driver, of your own life. He claimed you can be whoever you want to be if you cultivate your life properly. It is you alone who makes you become you.

Remember that, and 'reason well for a complete life', as the Greek philosopher Aristotle[2] urged.

Sadly, many people understand what the good life means for them too late in life for it to become a reality, and so they become burdened with regrets. Thankfully, I was introduced to the power of philosophy in my late forties. It was only then that I realised I had always been living a philosophical life but did not know it. That is, I was looking for and developing my own personal philosophy. Unknowingly, I have always been working towards having peace in my life and helping others find peace in theirs.

Where did it all start for me?

Since I lost friends in the Falklands War in 1982[3], out of respect for them I have grabbed life at every opportunity. I have used every experience good and bad throughout my life to help me lead a good life: because I can, and they cannot. It is up to you to tap into the people around you, the experiences that resonate with you, and to grow your life's philosophy from them. Trust me: if you do, you will not regret it.

Please recognise that you can have any life you want, if you truly want it. All you need to do is change the narrative (story) in your mind. Change negative or destructive thoughts into constructive, positive thoughts. You cannot achieve anything good while in a negative trajectory. Stop staying you cannot do things; instead, say what you *can* do. Change fear into hope, change hate into love and, most importantly, change doubt into belief.

Believe me, if you do this and take positive, constructive agency of your life, take control of your brain and give your life meaning, anything is possible and life becomes so much better and more enjoyable.

I have always been looking for the meaning to my life

On occasion I tried too hard to lead a good life. I tried too hard to give my life meaning, values and quality. Being ex-military and working in the fire and rescue service for many years, I have witnessed many hundreds of deaths: people taken far too early and too suddenly. Three examples come to mind: my best friend Budgie in the Royal Navy Fleet Air Arm, who died the day after the Falklands War ended in 1982, aged twenty-one; my wife Nicky who sadly died of cancer at the age of forty-six in 2016; and a very brave fire officer Paul Metcalfe who tragically died trying to rescue a stranger. The tragedy of those lives was they were taken far too soon. However, their gift to me was they taught me that life is precious and that the time I have is to be treasured. They taught me that I should enjoy each day and live life to my best and with a smile. This book is their legacy as they inspired me to write these *7 Rules to a Good Life*. Through feeling and living these 7 Rules, I want you to give yourself the best chance to live the good life now.

Life is short: the time to learn about your good life is now!

So become smart about what you do in life, as the only thing you cannot buy back is time. Once it is gone it is gone, and none of us really knows when it will end. The great thing is that your journey to the good life is available to you at any time, if you can take responsibility now. Grab your life while you can and, with the appropriate personal philosophy, you too can lead yourself to a good life. The Greek philosopher Seneca[4] said, 'Philosophy is the personal cure for identifying self or helping a healthy self.' But you have to want to develop your personal philosophy in life. So be like the Roman Emperor Marcus Aurelius[5] and be your own philosopher king or queen by always searching for the true you.

I designed the Live Life Smarter programme (set out in the *Appendix*) and this *7 Rules to a Good Life* framework to help you on your journey to be the best you can be, to be the person you want to be and to have the life you want to live. It will happen if you really want it. It is your life, and you only get the one! So don't wait: grab your life now and become the person you want to be.

As I write, I am into my sixty-second year. I am privileged and thankful that I have reached the place I want to be in life, helping people through my writing and through my coaching programme. After many experiences, good and bad, my simple life goal now is to help as many people as possible to get the best out of their lives. I want to help others to be smarter earlier in their lives. I want to help them avoid the mistakes I made. But, if I had not had such low experiences and losses, I would not now be writing this book. So, I see those sad events as my greatest learning gifts in life. This book can change your life, but only if you want it to. It is your choice; it is your decision to make. You will not regret it.

GET TO KNOW HOW YOUR BRAIN WORKS

I BELIEVE EVERYTHING YOU NEED for a positive life is inside your mind. I want to help you bring it out, so you can get as much out of your life as possible in a safe and constructive way. I will create a learning environment for you to master success in everything you do in whatever life you wish to lead.

The fact of life is: what you think, you will be. The brain is the greatest computer, but it is driven and developed through our experiences, thoughts and emotions which ultimately form our habits, attitudes and behaviours, and are actioned through the decisions we make and the actions we take (or do not take) across all parts of our lives. This learning journey starts at the moment we are born and ends only when we close our eyes for the last time.

Let me start with the big theme that flows through everything you do in life: **get to know how your brain works**. Whether you are in the lows of life or striving to achieve peak performance, controlling how you think is the key to a good life. This is called **agency** of mind.

Eminent gurus, coaches, philosophers and academics who will be presented throughout this book, believe that to achieve anything in life and be happy doing it, we must claim agency of our minds through our choices and decisions. The quality of our lives and the amount of risk we accept depends upon recognising that the responsibility for what happens is down to us and us alone.

Yes, life is full of ups and downs but, by embracing the *7 Rules to a Good Life*, you can minimise those lows and catch yourself quicker when life begins to drift. More importantly, you can help balance and re-set your brain with calmness, laughter and by changing the narrative in your head to a positive one. Laughter, comedy and not taking yourself too seriously offer a more balanced perspective. Humour helps your brain to relax and see things the way they are rather than through the prism of the stories you create from unclarified and unjustified thoughts and feelings. Your brain will play games with you if you let it: common sense is the golden nugget of reality. But why is common sense so uncommon? Because we may rely on what we *think* we know rather than what we *actually* know to be true.

To help you think clearly you can seek help from others. Peak performers seek out outstanding coaches. People living with depression may need counselling or cognitive behavioural therapy (CBT)[6]. But these supporters in life don't tell you what to do: they only create safe environments for you to think and make choices and decisions. Your life is *your* life, and you have the power to be anything you want to be.

My greatest achievement when my left brain met my right brain was looking after my wife Nicky who died after her battle with cancer in 2016. Nicky told me something profound the week before she passed away: 'when I die, please don't let two people die. Live your life to the full and be the best you can be, for me, but more for yourself. Do not stop loving life.'

From that moment, which consolidated my 2007 homeless experience (more on this later) and the loss of my friends in the Falklands War, I have strived to be the best I can be each day. I have completely removed anger from every element of my life. I celebrate the beauty of difference and embrace the power of the positive soul. I feel lucky to have reached peace and enlightenment in myself. It is a lovely place to be but, like all things in life, I cannot take it for granted. It takes hard work in continually developing my mind, behaviours and habits every day. I want you to be able to achieve this too. It is down to you. I will hold your hand, so to speak, and guide you through the *7 Rules to a Good Life*. And *you* will make decisions in your own life.

I will present thinkers who can help you in your journey to the good life

Viktor Emil Frankl[7], neurologist, psychiatrist, philosopher and writer, used the power of the brain to survive the Holocaust. He would tell you he was lucky to survive, but it was his attitude of mind that allowed him not to be beaten mentally while held captive as a Jewish prisoner during the Second World War. And it was this same attitude that helped him use those personal dark times to help others after. So please use his experiences to inspire you.

> 'Everything can be taken from a man but one thing: the last of the human freedoms; to choose one's attitude in any given set of circumstances, to choose one's own way.'
>
> —Viktor E. Frankl, Man's Search for Meaning

Viktor presented to his mind simple, positive psychological tools and frameworks that helped him be the person he wanted to be. He gave himself meaning even when all around him was dark.

My simple *7 Rules to a Good Life* will help you do this too. I have used all my forty-plus years of military, fire and rescue service, and academic experience, and my knowledge growth across those disciplines, to design and create an environment where you can live life smarter and achieve a good life. More importantly, I have used my experience of going from being highly successful in a variety of areas to losing everything in 2007 and spending two nights homeless on London's Euston Station.

I am in good company. Jim Rohn[8], the American entrepreneur, author and motivational speaker, became a millionaire at thirty, then lost it all at thirty-three. Through these experiences, he became a great life coach. At thirty-three he looked deep into himself and finally began to understand life. As a result, he took responsibility for himself and never looked back, always looking forward. This is what happened to me, too, when I found myself sleeping on Euston Station in the October of 2007 while still a serving officer in the British fire and rescue service.

I will place many people before you who can help you in your journey to the good life beyond my 7 Rules. It is important to remember here that this book and others can help you only to a point, as it is for you to do your own research and development across your life; never stop learning. You can start now by looking up the *Ultimate Jim Rohn Library*[8].

How agency works

Before I begin explaining the *7 Rules to a Good Life*, let me give you an insight into how agency works within your mind. But first a brave challenge to Albert Einstein's[9] alleged assertion:

Doing the same thing over and over again and expecting a different result each time = INSANITY

—Albert Einstein?

We don't see this only at an individual level – for example, when you drink too much or eat too much yet expect to stay the same weight and fitness – but on the world arena too with what's happening in Ukraine with Russia (at time of writing 2023). We still think as a species that going to war and being angry achieves something; it doesn't. We put so much effort into making weapons of war, mass destruction bombs and killing each other. Can you imagine if we put the same effort into eradicating poverty, hunger and criminality; into driving profound change for our planet's success, alongside prompting peace and togetherness? Do not think world politics has nothing to do with you: it does. And you can do your bit now, by living your own good life.

You can start by simply leading a true, honest and authentic life from this moment forward. You can change your mindset now and start to control how you think and what you do. Edward Thorndike,[10] an American psychologist, put forward a '**law of effect**' which stated that 'any behaviour that is followed by pleasant consequences is likely to be repeated, and any behaviour followed by unpleasant consequences is likely to be stopped'. The law of cause and effect states that, 'what you cause in your mind will affect you.' Charles Perrow[11] (Yale University) and Scott Snook[12] (Harvard University) talk about how you can 'drift' upwards in life and downwards. If you drift downwards, accidents are normal, because, when you move in that negative direction, you compound destructive emotions within the brain. However, when you create a positive momentum, that too has a compounding mental effect on your emotions and ultimately your habits and behaviour.

So, I believe Albert Einstein, or whoever really was the originator of that quote, missed a trick by couching it in negative terms. Here is my alternative:

Doing lots of different, intelligent, positive things to get results = SANITY

—Dave Armstrong

So why is understanding agency important?

If we look again at the 'law of effect', it tells us that you cannot achieve anything good with a negative or destructive emotion, feeling or thought. If you are negative, the effect will be negative. If you think positively, the effect will be positive. So, change the narrative in your mind to a positive one. However, it's not only about being positive, as Jordan Peterson[13], Canadian clinical psychologist and author, would suggest; it is about being 'intelligently' positive. This means having a positive mindset but also understanding why you need to have one through being honest with yourself and continually developing and challenging your skills, knowledge and experiences.

How you deal with the process of agency within your brain dictates your safety and happiness. It has a compounding, cumulating effect on your life and is seen externally through your habits and behaviours.

I believe that agency is developed through a three-stage continuous mental process:

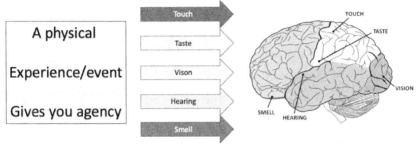

Agency Received

A physical

Experience/event

Gives you agency

Touch

Taste

Vison

Hearing

Smell

TOUCH

TASTE

VISION

SMELL HEARING

Driven by your senses into your body

NB: NOTHING ENTERS YOUR BODY APART FROM THROUGH YOUR SENSES!

Step 1: You RECEIVE agency via your bodily senses. If you cannot experience sight, sound, touch, taste and smell, you cannot fully learn, as outside information cannot enter your body. Nothing enters your body and into your mind other than through your senses. This is a simple fact from birth to death. Edward Thorndike spent nearly his entire career at Teachers College, Columbia University. His work and passion were seated in the psychology of the learning process and led to the development of the 'law of effect' principle. In the field of behaviourism, this is known as *operant conditioning*, whereby the body responds to an external stimulus. Formed the basis for our understanding of how we educate people today, this is linked to my concept of Receiving Agency.

Think about this: if you let yourself enter a toxic environment, your senses will pick up what is around you.

So, open your mind to a constructive and positive environment not a destructive and negative one, because the second part of the agency process, *feeling of agency*, is driven by what your senses pick up. Through those five senses, it enters your body and lands in the brain. A simple example of this is where someone offers you a cake. You see the cake, you hear the voice of the person offering you the cake, you can smell the cake, and you can touch the cake. You are receiving agency via your senses. If you're on a controlled diet, do not eat the cake. Be strong. Move away from the cake.

If other people say you cannot do a particular thing, you will never amount to anything, you are ugly or you don't belong, you can hear and experience those comments; but once you receive that information from another, it is not for them to tell you how to respond, it is for you to decide that for yourself. Think about this: the basic way of dealing with risk is by taking yourself away from it, removing or reducing it. So, make sure the experiences you afford yourself help you rather than hinder your personal growth. Be smart and put yourself in a place where people have your best interests at heart, want to support you and believe in you. Remember, it is you who has placed yourself in a position to receive these moments of agency. These moments are commonly known as an experience, where you let information enter your body. So, choose wisely what you let yourself experience. This sounds so simple and obvious, but, if you don't seek to understand how sensations enter the body, and, more importantly, if you don't have appreciation of where the sensations in your mind come from, it is harder to control the next step, the feeling of agency.

Feel Agency

Worked on by your brain through:

The battle between your Yin (left) & Yang (right)!

Step 2: You FEEL agency. This is the 'sixth sense' concerning how you deal with all the information you feed your brain from your five physical senses. Once an experience enters the body through your senses, the mind starts working on your emotions, feelings and thoughts. The brain has many complex processes but I will attempt to simplify this process of agency. The brain in very simple terms has two halves, the left side (which can be compared to the philosophical concept of Yin, meaning Order) and the right side (which has been likened to the concept of Yang, Chaos). The left is the analytical and logical half; it controls cognitive functions. Cognition is the mental process by which we acquire knowledge and understanding through thought, experience and the information received from our five senses. The right brain is interpreted as the creative and innovative half, the more fluid of the two sides.

Yin & Yang

In broad terms, the brain's two halves will battle it out for what to do with all the sensory information they receive. This is the *feeling* of agency. This is the area of the agency process where you are required to be strong, to take responsibility for your judgement and the decision you are about to make.

WARNING

Do not wilfully lie to yourself; don't kid yourself. The good angel on your shoulder is telling you to do the right thing: keep to your diet; do NOT eat that cake. However, if you do not control your mind, the devil on your other shoulder will lead you to deny your responsibility for the judgements you take and will lead you to 'wilfully lie' by telling yourself that eating just one cake will not do any harm. Whether that is true or not, if you choose to be weak and succumb, the compounding effect of repeating that action will be that you will eat the cake and put on weight, producing more negative compounding effects within your behaviours and habits. However, if you are strong and take responsibility for your situation, you will decline the cake and you will lose weight. This analogy can be transferred across any situation you find yourself in. Do not wilfully lie, as the only person you are lying to is YOU.

At this point the third part of the agency process kicks in.

Take Agency

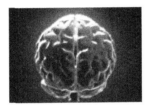

Decision Time

Choice Time

It's the action you **Take** or **Don't Take**

Step 3: You TAKE agency. This part of the agency process is a singular moment in time, known as a decision, whereas the feeling of agency process in Step 2 is more fluid and subjective: your thinking time.

Remember this: the agency you are about to take is yours and the responsibility that goes with it is also yours; so, choose wisely. You either eat the cake or don't eat the cake: the choice is yours; the decision is yours. Whether you listen to toxic language or supportive language, the choice is yours, the decision is yours. It is a singular moment because the action you take (the decision you make) in that moment is what matters; the future will dictate whether it was a good one or not. This is what elite athletes, business people and academics live by. It is the moment you are in that matters: it is this run, this throw, this swim, this deal; it is this project, this game you are playing now. They know it doesn't matter what has gone on in the past nor what might happen in the future. It is what you do now only that is important; and what comes from that either helps you or hinders you. However, from the agency you have taken in the past, you do have a chance to self-moderate if it doesn't go so well as expected. If you learn effectively from the past, you can improve yourself and/or your team in the future. So, once you have eaten the cake, that decision cannot be changed. I call it the **singular moment**, where you move from feeling agency to taking agency. This is why my **Rule 4 to a Good Life** is focussed on keeping learning. This moment between feeling agency and taking agency is what I call the 'gateway to learning'. You will decide to either keep the gate shut through negative emotion or open it and develop your life's positive trajectory.

MIND THE GAP

THE GAP WE ARE LOOKING AT HERE is created by the compounding effects of the positive or negative habits that define your day-to-day behaviours. 'Compounding' is the cumulative effect of your good or bad behaviours, with the trajectory of those behaviours having an impact on whether you live a good life or not.

What is compounding?

Compounding has two clear trajectories; a negative and a positive direction. It is the act of combining, the repeating of a good or a bad habit that leads to a behaviour. If we think in financial terms, compounding interest over years is the golden thread of sustained wealth. It is the positive accumulation of compound interest that creates that wealth. When we talk about compounding within the *7 Rules to a Good Life*, it is for you to control the trajectory of the compounding effect across all areas of your life. So, make sure it has a positive outcome.

Scott Snook talks about the negative and positive effects of compounding. To follow my cake example: if you keep denying or excusing what you do through wilfully lying to yourself that it is okay to eat the cake when it is not, you will drift in a negative direction and put on weight. As Charles Perrow asserts, accidents are then normal and should be expected from that negative trajectory. If you eat too much and have a heart attack or other illness associated with overeating, this is inevitable as you chose to ignore moments of past agency.

As an alcoholic you may convince yourself you will have just one more for the road; as a gambler one more bet will get your money back, and as a thief you will take on just one more job. If you see or hear someone being bullied, you might say it has nothing to do with you. Or you might falsify a record to make your job easier, because you have been set unachievable targets. The compounding effect of these actions, or inactions, causes you to drift in life. You cannot achieve anything with negative and destructive agency. So, address the warning of the known risk, and deal with the agency moment you received in the first instance.

In a work environment, if you ignore warnings from staff that equipment is becoming unsafe, if you continually ignore high-risk issues being raised by others, you can expect tragedy to happen. An accident or disaster is built from an initial risk ignored. Examples of this include the tragic and totally avoidable 2017 Grenfell Fire in London UK[14] in which 72 people died, and the Hillsborough football stadium disaster[15] in 1997 that killed 97 Liverpool supporters. The warning signs were there many years before those disasters happened, but they were all ignored for one reason or another. The compounding effects of avoidance and ignorance are formed within our individual habits and behaviours. When this happens within a group or team, there is potential for exponential growth of avoidance and ignorance.

Please think about this: simple accidents to disasters all stem from a risk that is ignored in its first instance. The warning signs are all there and once ignored the compounding effect will take place. Drift in the mind will lead to an unsure life, so mind that gap growing.

Anything is Possible

Compounding *gain* through taking positive, constructive agency will lead to life improvement. So, if you do not eat the cake, you lose weight; if you go to the gym and exercise in some form, you get fitter and, if you deal with the bully, your workplace becomes a safer more productive place. If you do not falsify records, your standards and quality will improve and your risks reduce. Dealing with agency in the mind has a compounding cumulative effect. Always remember, everything you do leading up to the moment you take agency and make a decision is what creates that moment from your feeling of agency. Make sure you feed your brain with, and open your senses to, appropriate experiences that will not hurt you. A fantastic book to consider here for a more in-depth view of how the brain functions is *A Path through the Jungle* by Professor Steve Peters[16]. The book includes an insight into his work around *The Chimp Paradox*[16]. Steve explains how the brain works psychologically and neurologically using three notional areas: the computer, the human and the chimp; the computer being the process part of the brain, which is fed by the human and the chimp. The human brain is seen as the logical, structured area and the reality part of the brain, while the chimp is seen as the naughty trouble-maker within the brain, the reactional, emotional part of the brain (which sometimes does have its advantages). Later, I will explain this in greater depth, but it is useful to flag his book up now.

Remember, by compounding all negative agency, anything can be destroyed. Compounding all our positive agency, anything is possible. Turn hate into love. Stop staying you cannot do things and say instead: *what can I do?* Change fear into hope, and more importantly change doubt into belief. Believe me, if you do this and take positive constructive agency of your life, anything is possible and life becomes so much better. I know what I choose: I take SANITY over INSANITY – sorry, Mr Einstein.

The Poison and Danger of the Wilful Lie

The wilful lie is when you intentionally or unintentionally lie to yourself. The wilful lie is set in the mind. Intentionally lying to yourself is the worst of the two but the easiest to control, as it is a deliberate act within the mind to not deal with the truth that you face. It is an act of choice. It is you and only you who has consciously ignored that something is not right. It the conscious deliberate act of doing something that you believe may have adverse consequences, but you choose to ignore them. Like eating a cake on a diet, smoking and knowing the effects on your body, having a bet knowing that you can't risk that money, or manipulating and then submitting a work record in work knowing it is incorrect but makes your life easier in the short term.

The compounding effect of a wilful lie is seen through stubbornness or maliciousness. The greatest of all wilful lies is *I know everything*. Here is a reality check: there is always something to learn, something you can develop. The day you stop learning is the day you close your eyes for the last time. When people claim to be the best or wisest, they are wilfully lying to themselves. Strong teams, great people and peak performers across time know it is not for them to say these things, but for others to recognise. They know that arrogance and complacency are the killers of improvement.

Then there is the unintentional lie, the subtle, uncomfortable feeling you have that something is not right. This is sometimes linked to bystander mentality and allows other people to manipulate you. Bystander mentality means simply letting things happen, but in fact you make a choice to go along with the status quo. This is an active choice. If you do not say no, intervene or choose another direction, you are actively accepting the situation or decisions that are being made and taken on your behalf by another. Yes, this is a hard one to deal with as the consequences for you at that moment can be great, and to stand up and address what is going on can be difficult. Can you imagine all the good German people hearing the orders of Adolf Hitler[17] during the 1930s and 1940s and having that uncomfortable feeling that something was not right, but being too scared or powerless to do something about it? Do not hide from the fact that, if you feel something is not right, doing nothing at all is allowing the compounding effect of the wilful lie to flourish and embed itself into your day-to-day life. Whistle-blowing is now protected by law, so that anyone can, if they are brave enough, put their head above the parapet of what might be going on, to raise their hand at something that needs to be addressed or talked about.

There is also a law in the UK called the Corporate Manslaughter and Corporate Homicide Act 2007[18] which calls to account any company that has lied, chosen knowingly to ignore risks, kept itself ignorant of the law or consciously cheated, or created a work environment that prioritises quick-fix profits over safety, and in doing any of these things has caused an employee's death. When such things do happen, everyone comes out of the woodwork after the accident or disaster and is happy to say, '*See, that was so obvious. We all knew that would happen one day*'. When people react this way, it is the tragic result of lots of wilful lies having lain dormant for weeks, months or years, and allowed to have a compounding effect on behaviours and habits.

Another great wilful lie is anger. Anger is the end-product of personal frustration when you either do not know something, do not have the skills, or you are not experienced enough to deal with what is placed in front of you. It is like what some people deem as failure. To me, there is no such thing as failure: it is simply a moment in time when something has gone wrong; and it is an opportunity to be honest and stop wilfully lying to yourself. It is a moment when something did not go as well as it should have done, or when you know you could have done better. Therefore, it is the time to recognise you need more knowledge, skill development or extra experience so that you can improve and 'go again.' Over my lifetime, I know it was in the dark, so-called bad, times when I took responsibility for them and removed anger from my soul, that I found a way to 'go again'. Those moments of 'go again' are open to us all. They are our *gateway to learning* which I will talk about later.

Be your own 'point person'

During the Falklands War in 1982 I was fortunate not to perform the role of 'point' too often. The 'point' is the chosen person from a group or team. It is the person who goes first through a dangerous or hostile area. They are the front person: on point. Their role is to go first and, if they see anything concerning, dangerous or that they have doubts about, they raise their hand in the air with a clenched fist. Once the others see the clenched fist, they stop. You do not ignore the clenched fist, no matter what or who you are. In a war situation you can die if you do ignore the clenched fist. If you are arrogant, stubborn or think you know best, you might ignore the signal. I have been fortunate to have good relationships with IED (improvised explosive device) and EOD (explosive ordnance disposal) experts.

Me (left) with an IED & EOD expert — 2000

They know one mistake, or one instance of ignoring a known risk, and you will die. When the 'point' person sees something and you ignore them, that bomb or booby trap will go off whether you like it or not.

You may be thinking: *what has this got to do with me?* It has everything to do with you as you are your own life's 'point' person. What are your clenched fist moments? Do you respect them or wilfully lie to yourself about them? Be your own 'point' person and make sure your personal bombs do not go off.

The clenched fist signal for stop —
danger or questions to be asked.

Poignantly, this clenched fist is used by many groups to highlight injustice today.

To conclude, what is the wilful lie and why is it dangerous? **The wilful lie will attack your values and peace of mind.** Wilful lies are feelings or emotions that you need to address and control. Remove anger and the word 'failure' from your mind. Put you hand up to yourself and think about the choices you need to make and actions you need to take now. Develop a new skill, develop new knowledge, or embark on a new or alternative experience. Once you do that, you can and will 'go again' in life, giving yourself the best chance to live a good life.

Eradicate negativity and drive your dreams forward

As Stephen Covey[19] would suggest, first things first. What you think, you will be. This is how the brain works. Sounds so simple. However, many people do not accept or are ignorant of this simple fact and so struggle in life. On the other hand, successful and happy people embrace this simple mental position and lead an intelligent, positive life. Buddhism claims that 'the cause of all pain and suffering is ignorance'.

The Dalai Lama[20] suggests the art of happiness is through self-determination and self-love. To me, it is all that and so much more, as you may not yet have been given the opportunity to look at yourself safely. You may not yet have been offered the simple mental tools to work with in a positive environment.

Most humans do not like being wrong or to be found to be wrong. Many deem this to be failure, and experience negativity, frustration, denial and anger as a consequence. As you progress through this book, I want you to be positive in everything you do and remove the word 'failure' from your vocabulary. Eradicate negativity and drive your dreams forward.

REFLECTION MOMENT

There is no such thing as failure when something happens. The thoughts that surround such feelings is an indication that you lack some skills, knowledge or experience. So, embrace those moments and don't be fearful of them. See them as gifts to yourself to improve. In simple terms they are the moments to open your 'gateway to learning'; so always be ready to open that gate.

Think about this: do things happen in life randomly? No, they do not. As highlighted earlier, Thorndike's, scientific presentation of the Law of Effect is set around cause and effect. If we look back in time, Aristotle called it the Law of Causality, and it is key to how we gain or drift in life. You think negatively, negative things will happen. However, if you think positively, you feed your brain and positive things will happen.

WARNING

Making this happen is solely down to you. Here is the hard part: yes, people can influence you, people can coerce you into doing things you may not agree with or believe in; but the bottom line is it is you and only you who can action your feelings, thoughts and emotions through the life decisions you make. I am not saying this is easy. It is not. I too have had massive ups and massive downs in life: but each up and each down is why I can now write my *7 Rules to a Good Life.*

I was lucky to have a nurturing environment as a child with loving parents. In addition, at the age of 17 I joined the Royal Navy Fleet Air Arm. Although I am now a defensive pacifist, I do fully acknowledge that my personal values in life were set back then: integrity, honesty, belief in myself, belief in others. I learned early to control my emotions, never stop learning and never stop growing, to embrace difference and recognise that working together is more powerful than working apart. Most importantly, I learned at that tender age that anything is possible in my life and that it is me and only me who is responsible for making things happen. I was so lucky and grateful. It was instilled in me during my military time that, when something did not go too well, you reflected upon yourself and looked at what knowledge, skills or experience you lacked and then did something about it. In the military, I knew people always had my back, as my friends do today. That does not mean only being nice to me, but being honest with me no matter what. Sometimes friends and colleagues would say things I did not want to hear but, on every occasion, it was a true position they saw that I did not. I was always encouraged to open my own 'gateway to learning' and this gave me the belief that everything and anything was possible in life.

My challenge to you: keep your mind open to progress and positivity.

An open mind leads to progress and when you do open your mind it is a wonderful place to go. I am not saying it is easy, as you become vulnerable, but it is only when you feel vulnerability that true learning takes place. These *7 Rules to a Good Life* will help you open your mind without fear and will offer you a safe place to reflect upon yourself. They will help you to stop looking for defeat and will drive you towards seeking success in life. Whether you are a young person job-hunting, a member of a professional task force, a stay-at-home parent, a highflying chief executive or a struggling athlete, **my challenge to you is to open your own gateway to learning with me and I will help you become the person you always wanted to be.**

Some critics may say these *7 Rules* are too simplistic. They will be missing the point: the *7 Rules to a Good Life* create a template from which anyone can start to design their own pathway in life. I am not a fan of certificates, so there is no accredited standard to my framework. Even a PhD means nothing if you do not do something with it. A certificate is only a moment of time to remember what you studied, and a tick in the box on a job application. It is what you do for yourself *after* that moment in time that gives a paper qualification value. This book is no different. I want you to not only *read* about the framework but to *apply* the **7 Rules** to your life (if you choose to). Therefore my *7 Rules* are simple, memorable and can be held in your mind and brought forward at a moment's notice.

So, the *7 Rules to a Good Life* are designed for you with full respect to the thinkers who have influenced me. I have tried to encapsulate all that wisdom and condense it in a simple easy-to-use way. Yes, I am a reading nerd and a learning nerd; I never stop, and I recognise there is always something new to experience and learn from. I keep my senses open so I can constantly receive moments of agency. I have a hands-free speaker and virtual assistant device (more commonly known as Alexa) with an audiobook app in every room of my house and even in my car. Sadly, it took me nearly forty-five years to recognise that my learning goes through the roof when I listen. This is why I have designed my *7 Rules to a Good Life* coaching programme to tap into all learning styles, whether you are a listener (auditory learner), watcher (visual learner), doer (kinaesthetic learner), or a mix of all three.

The safe environment I aim to create within these pages will encourage you to form your own habits and behaviours, so that you can use them on a daily basis. This book is not about telling you or training you: it is showing that you can feel and see your life for yourself. There will be no walking over hot coals. I simply want you to wake up each morning, feel alive and be excited about the day ahead. From such daily successes, anything is possible.

What happens next?

I will now introduce and explain the *why* and *how* of each of my *7 Rules to a Good Life*. Within each rule I will present frameworks, theories and models to give you a real-life understanding of that rule and how to apply it to your life straight away. Each rule will have clear references to outstanding people who have developed this area of human behaviour and philosophy of life.

It is then up to you to choose those frameworks, stories, theories, experiences, models and references that resonate with you and apply them to your own unique life experiences. I am not telling you to do anything about your life, I am simply giving you a heads up for you to make decisions for yourself.

I have concluded each rule with a challenge. Use these Good Life Challenges to give yourself goals that you believe apply to you. This is the key to a good life: to take responsibility and give yourself direction and meaning through setting yourself challenges.

Finally, I encourage you all to TAKE AGENCY at the end of each chapter. Be aware you will have an academic debate within your own mind; as it is necessary to decide where to position yourself. However, there are differing, often opposing, viewpoints to balance. For example, the German philosopher Nietzsche criticises and positions himself differently from the Greek philosopher Socrates[21]. For anyone trying to better themselves, this can be confusing: who do you believe, who do you follow? My *7 Rules* are not for debate, as I believe each is embedded within most neurologists', philosophers' and psychologists' thinking. For example, every single coach, philosopher and psychologist I have read or listened to will tell you that taking responsibility for yourself is the first rule to personal growth. The same goes for the idea that you cannot achieve anything without giving what you do meaning (direction), and the assertion that you should never stop learning as it is part of life's journey. If you do start to debate in your head, you can confuse yourself as each thinker is excellent at arguing their case and they all have merit. So, for each rule, the TAKE AGENCY moment is down to you, and you are responsible for accepting the presented ideas or not. Choose wisely and keep challenging yourself each day.

Here is a quote that has resonated with me since I first read it in 1997 in the book *Fuzzy Management: Contemporary Ideas and Practices at Work* by Keith Grint[22], a professor at Oxford University specialising in organisation behaviour and leadership who spent many years working in various positions across a number of industries before switching to an academic career. So, Keith has an appreciation of the linkage between theory and practice. This quote is from one of his students:

'Theory is where you know everything, and nothing works. Practice is where everything works but nobody knows why. Here we combine theory and practice: nothing works and nobody knows why."

Develop your knowledge of theory and keep practising and growing your skills in the real world. If you do that, you will bring your left and right brains closer together, which gives you the best chance to ensure that everything works and (more importantly) you know why within a good life. The *7 Rules to a Good Life* are a great foundation to build that upon.

I hope you enjoy this learning journey. Take responsibility for your destiny from this point forward. Never rest on your laurels, always keep learning and always keep growing. Keep calm, think through and enjoy whatever you do with a smile. Because if you do, you will live a good life from this point forward on whatever path you choose to go down. The power is with you.

LIVE LIFE
SMARTER

7
RULES
TO A
GOOD
LIFE

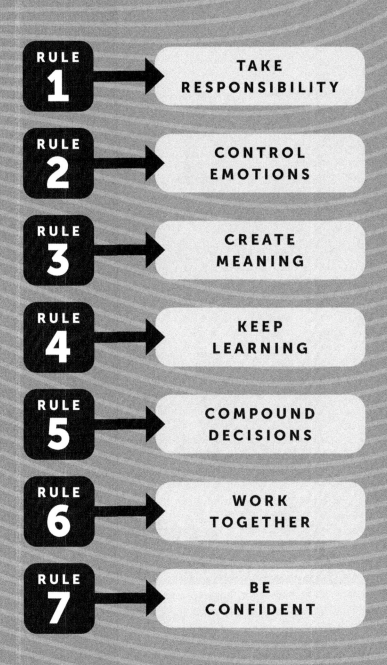

RULE 1 → TAKE RESPONSIBILITY

RULE 2 → CONTROL EMOTIONS

RULE 3 → CREATE MEANING

RULE 4 → KEEP LEARNING

RULE 5 → COMPOUND DECISIONS

RULE 6 → WORK TOGETHER

RULE 7 → BE CONFIDENT

RULE 1
TO A GOOD LIFE:

TAKE RESPONSIBILITY

Why take responsibility?

You won't have the life you want if you don't take responsibility for it.

If you do not recognise that the responsibility for your life is yours, your life will not be yours. It is only when you take responsibility for yourself that your life will change in a positive, smart and sustainable way. Once you understand that and have you own moments of profound 'self-realisation' your life will change for ever and you will never look back. Unless of course you become complacent with your responsibility and that too can happen anywhere and at any time. Life is never plain sailing as you will have your ups and downs, but to develop good habits, Tony Robbins[23] would suggest you must anchor those habits into your behaviours. Then the ups will be greater than the downs. Jim Rohn, the American motivational speaker who greatly influenced

Tony Robbins, suggests everyone should take responsibility for their personal philosophy if they want to lead a happy and successful life.

For example, if you spend too much and you are knowingly spending outside your means, your life becomes financially unbalanced. Know that it is you who has allowed this to happen, no one else. Do you want your income to grow so you can spend more? Then take responsibility for making this change happen. Whether or not you enjoy your work is something you can control. If you do not enjoy your job, change it, or at least plan a strategy to change it.

The quality of your friends is also your responsibility: you can choose to engage with them or not. Friends will either support you or will not have your best interests at heart. So, stay with them or remove them from your life. Do you share your life with your soulmate and best friend who you love? Or are you in a toxic relationship and incompatible with each other? Recognise it is your responsibility to stay or go.

You are what you are, you live the way you live, you behave the way you behave, and you think the way you think. Take responsibility for it all and own it.

Look at yourself now in the mirror and start to take responsibility. Everyone can do this, there is no excuse. If you are in the lows of life, you too can take responsibility for where you find yourself mentally, but this is a difficult ask as you may not yet see the route out. You may need help, and the responsibility you take at this stage may be as simple as accepting the situation you are in and putting your hand out to ask for support from another. So be 'on point' in your life. For peak performers, the issue here is to keep on taking responsibility to maintain the level you are at and, if possible, improve your performance further. No matter what stage of life you are in, the first step is owning and taking responsibility for the life you have at this moment in time. As I did on Euston station in 2007, grab your life, take responsibility for the situation you are in, and life will become so much better. You can do this at any time.

Euston station concourse — London

The moment of taking responsibility for self is not a quick fix; it is a journey in life that we all take. Most people who have had major success also hit major disappointments. One of the dangers in business is growing too fast and too soon as most companies struggle when this happens. This is the same in your personal life. Therefore, you must keep reflecting upon yourself throughout your life and put self-responsibility central to your personal philosophy. The more you repeat this central first principle, the easier it becomes as it will be embedded within your daily habits and behaviours. I was lucky when I joined the Royal Navy Fleet Air Arm in 1979 as it was then that my values and principles were instilled in me. The fact that I ended up on Euston station in 2007 was solely down to me, because I got complacent and confused, and allowed myself to be influenced and misguided by those around me. But the bottom line was I let them get to me and let my core value of self-responsibility slide.

So *why* should you own your profound 'self-realisation' moment of taking responsibility for yourself? Because once you have that in your habits and behaviours your life will be fundamentally better and you will be taking the first step towards living life smarter, to living a good life. You will be setting a strong behavioural foundation around your acceptance of personal responsibility that will give you the best chance to make anything you wish for or any dream possible.

Taking responsibility for self is a state of mind. It means you have taken up the position of being responsible for you and everything you do in life. You recognise and own that you are the one person responsible for you. Taking responsibility for yourself gives you the ability and authority to act and decide on your own future. Many call that true personal independence, personal sovereignty, and even self-enlightenment.

Maslow's (Advanced) Hierarchy of Needs: A model for understanding

Abraham Harold Maslow[24], the American psychologist, suggested it is in making sure that you take responsibility, that you ensure all your needs are met, and this helps you to transcend to a good and happy life.

Maslow presented his steps in life to help each one of us to an understanding of all our needs, which he classed primary and secondary needs. He encouraged us to build upon our primary basic needs to set a foundation whereby all individual needs are met so we can 'transcend' to a good and happy life. His original hierarchy of needs model is well known. However, what is less well known is that he developed his model further after a conversation with Viktor Frankl, and this was only published after his death in 1970. The conversations between these two amazing human beings help us to access their knowledge and experience through their work, allowing us to get the best out of our lives irrespective of how dark our current situations are.

Viktor Frankl's insight into his life experiences and subsequent work after he and his family were forced to move to the Terezin Ghetto, and then unbelievably survived Auschwitz concentration camp, is a gift to humanity. Although I focus on Maslow's work in the next section, here once again I highly recommend Frankl's book *Man's Search for Meaning*.

So, take responsibility for everything in your life and recognise it is you and only you who is responsible for it. If you understand what taking responsibility means and embed it into your life, the benefits are enormous.

How do you take responsibility?

There are many theories, models or frameworks out there and you can argue that one is better than another. Take Herzberg's[25] Two-Factor Theory. Unlike Maslow, Herzberg held that primary needs were the hygiene factors in life and secondary needs were the motivators. People through time have argued around the same behavioural debates by presenting what they know in different models, theories and frameworks. You can get embroiled in 'this theory says this, and that theory says that', but you will be missing the point, which is that, to help yourself to live a good life, you need structure and a pathway to grow. It is up to you to take responsibility for yourself and form your own structures so that, as Tony Robbins suggests, you can anchor your habits and behaviours in whichever theory or model resonates with you. So let me introduce you to Abraham Maslow's developed hierarchy of needs.

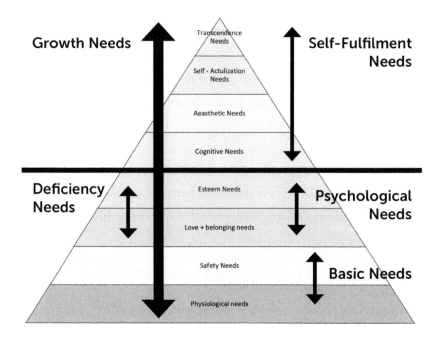

Maslow's advanced version of his Hierarchy of Needs.

Physiological needs

Take responsibility for your physiological needs. These are the basic biological requirements for your survival, and include the air you breathe, the food and drink you put inside yourself, the home you create, clothing you wear, warmth, sex and sleep. These foundations of life are set around how you manage your work life balance which I will talk about later. If these needs are not satisfied, the human body cannot function properly. Maslow considered physiological needs the most important, as all the other needs become secondary until these needs are met. These needs are the foundation in your life and are key to having a balanced life.

Safety needs

Take responsibility for your safety needs. This level of need concerns your personal security and safety within the life you live. These needs are fulfilled primarily by yourself and the responsibility you attach to them. However, the quality and safety of your life can be supported by those you bring into your life for help and guidance. This will include family and friends, and all the people within your work environment. Safety needs cover many areas, including your emotional stability, financial freedom and the laws and values you uphold as your standards. From this solid or weak foundation, lots of benefits can be achieved or risks increased. The benefits include the stability you have where you live, what you earn, how you spend, your general health and the freedom it gives you.

I will present to you, shortly, the Wheel of a Balanced Life. Understanding and using this tool can help you enormously with your safety needs and with the most basic needs in Maslow's hierarchy, physiological needs.

Love and belonging needs

Take responsibility for your love and belonging needs. This is the third level of human needs introduced by Maslow in his updated version. Belonging refers to the human emotional need for interpersonal relationships, affiliation, connectedness and being part of a group or team. Love and belonging needs resonate around your friendships and relationships and involve intimacy, trust, and acceptance in others, including the receiving and giving of thought, care, affection and love. This need is linked to self-esteem: if you can't love yourself, it is hard to love others properly. You should not merely fit into a team; you should *belong* in it. So do not confuse love with lust, and do not confuse belonging with fitting in. When you are in a relationship: do not make do if it is based on lust and quick fun, as it will not last. If you want a long-lasting relationship, make sure that person opposite you is your best friend, not only in the good times but at the low points. Make sure they are someone who stands by you because they want to, not because they have to; someone you can laugh with and cry with; someone you respect and who respects you despite all the differences you and they may have. Unconditional love is the most powerful of all loves. Some people, however, use the unconditional in an abusive, controlling way. Unconditional love is a natural, organic and non-demanding feeling, because when you give it to another your love gets stronger rather than weaker.

It is the same with an outstanding team: once you realise that you have love and belonging in a team you work together as one. Each person is respected and loved for what they do, from cook to chief executive. If each person in a team is respected and loved, they have self-esteem and a sense of belonging within that team. This is what my **Rule 6: Working Together** is about. Working together, feeling loved and knowing you belong, is far better than feeling outcast from the group that are working apart. When you have this met this need anything is possible and everything is achievable.

Esteem needs

Take responsibility for your esteem needs. The fourth level in Maslow's hierarchy is set around your self-worth and personal respect. Many people today find this difficult, particularly in this celebrity world of so-called perfection, fabricated looks and false lives. Only take responsibility for who you are, and change yourself from a position of pride, not insecurity. Develop your self-esteem from your own perspective on life, not based on what the media show you. Your esteem needs are set across two areas: have esteem for yourself and have self-esteem regarding your reputation or the respect others feel for you.

After the Falklands War, I lost my self-esteem totally, as I had feelings of guilt that I had survived when many of my friends, including my best friend, did not make it. So, up until 2007, I struggled with my self-esteem. The outward presentation I gave was that of a soul angry with myself, and I saw others in poor light for not realising how lucky they were when they had every opportunity available to them to live any life they wanted. I saw people constantly moaning or cheating on the backs of others to get the lives they wanted.

This decline happens to many military veterans who go to war and serve their country, putting their lives on the line: they quickly lose their self-esteem once they leave. They return to 'real life,' where they find a world that to them is false, deceitful, full of backstabbers and over-flowing with people of self-interest. It is interesting to me that military personnel who return home *physically* injured have, and quite rightly so, all the support they need. But for those of us who return uninjured physically, though scarred mentally, there is little or no help, so we have to deal alone with building up our self-esteem again in a different world from the one we left when we were healthy. You only have to look around every city in our country to see the many homeless military veterans who find a life in a doorway on a street.

Please don't think us veterans are special: it is the same for anyone who has built themselves up and then been built up by others when they reach the top of their chosen fields of expertise. A prime example of this might be a young premier league footballer or American basketball player. Once that floor of usefulness to others is gone, the rug is pulled from under you, and that is when your self-esteem is taken away in an instant. Hence why many people decline rapidly in retirement, as they deem themselves to suddenly have no direction or responsibility once work has gone. The hard part is that, when this happens, no one seems to care.

The saving grace for me was that I had built a previous foundation of solid principles and values that will never go away and so I was able to regroup and 'go again,' as all great sports teams say. That is why my **Rule 5: Compounding Decisions** throughout your life is so crucial to starting again. Continual development, setting up a foundation of authentic and honest habits and behaviours, affords you the ability to catch yourself when you begin to drift too much, helping you to stay ahead of your life's curve. The bottom line for my change in 2007 was that it was me who had allowed that drift to go on too long and me who had allowed myself to fall down my destructive curve in life; nearly to suicide. So, I took responsibility for myself and, thankfully, the penny dropped before it was too late. I had lost my self-esteem, but my first step was to recognise no one could help me except me. From that point, I focussed on rebuilding my self-esteem and, by taking responsibility for myself as I was taught in the Royal Navy, I could 'go again'. That was the single best decision of my life. And it will be yours if you ever get to those dark places.

From every unique story of life, from every walk of life, people will have doubts, negative thoughts about themselves. Just remember: the beauty of life is we are all different, so celebrate your difference. You are beautifully unique: you simply need to grab that and feel it. The beauty of life is we all have a part to play in this world. Some want to go to the moon; most want to have a happy life with family and friends around them; each role is equal in value. So, build your own self-esteem, and, from that, esteem for you will be built naturally with others. If you do it with a smile in your heart, then the world is your oyster, and anything is possible. This is why my final **Rule 7** is: **be confident** and enjoy all you do!

Cognitive needs

Aesthetic needs are built from your cognitive needs. So, now take responsibility for these. Cognitive needs are about you being open to new experiences, having the desire and ability to investigate and discover new feelings and emotions. This is built upon a foundation of continual learning around all elements of your life. Fulfilling your cognitive needs means you have a better understanding of the world around you. More importantly, fulfilling your cognitive needs means you have a better understanding of yourself. Taking responsibility for your cognitive needs gives you a deeper understanding of how you need to change and of how embracing change is key to your future success and happiness. By nurturing your cognitive development, you will create a solid personal foundation for all other needs to be fulfilled. Hence my **Rule 4: Keep Learning**. For me, this is the key need to take responsibility for because it gives you stability and sustainability for what you do now and want to do next. Compounding (gradually growing) your cognitive area is the engine that drives the quality of your life and reduces the risks in your life. The key here regarding taking responsibility for your cognitive needs is this: continually growing your skills, knowledge and experiences will give stability across your life and allow you to have a go at and achieve anything you want to do or be in life.

Aesthetic needs

These were introduced in the refresh of Maslow's hierarchy of needs. To achieve self-actualization, Maslow realised you need to have positive and beautiful visualisations within new experiences and adventures that motivate you to continue to self-actualization. This need, when fulfilled, leads you to feelings of integrity with a commitment to take things to another level. The word 'visualisation' can be seen as insubstantial to some: it is not. You actually visualise every moment of the day and throughout your life, and maybe without realising you are doing it. You wake up and think: what am I going to do today? If you go on holiday, you don't simply go somewhere, you visualise which places you would like to visit. When you buy a car, you visualise what type and what colour. When you buy a house, you visualise where you want to live. You visualise what career you want, what success you want and what fun you want. So, appreciate visualisation is not only for the visionaries in life: each one of us does it every day, at every moment in the day. Let's have those powerful visualisations. The more powerful and simple your goal, the better chance you have of success. The more complicated the goal, the more chance you will not achieve it. So, **take responsibility (Rule 1)** and **create clear meaning (Rule 3)** in everything you do, and start your journey by addressing your aesthetic needs and creating positive and beautiful visualisations. This will direct you to have new experiences and adventures that motivate you to continue to self-actualization.

Self-actualization needs

Self-actualization is the highest level in Maslow's original hierarchy of needs, and refers to the realisation of a person's potential, self-fulfilment and the ability to achieve peak performances across their life experiences. Some examples might be winning a gold medal at the Olympics, or your child leaving university with a first-class degree, or running a successful business. Other examples might be baking the best cake or meal you possibly can for your family, or simply sitting in an open space with your partner and letting the world go by knowing it doesn't get better than this. Maslow describes this level as the desire to accomplish everything you want in life, to become the person you want to be in any given moment of time. The greatest self-actualization is happiness and contentment with yourself. Now, *that* is a challenge.

Transcendence needs

Taking responsibility to aim for your transcendence level in life means you can gradually move forward and reach contentment, happiness and enlightenment, and on your deathbed you will be smiling, without regrets, happy with what you have done. Maslow's Transcendence Level is the calmness within your soul after your reach self-actualization. It is the very highest level of human consciousness and can be related to enlightenment and inner peace. How you achieve this is by taking responsibility for everything you do in your life now, and continually moving forward. Grow your life in a positive trajectory, riding the ups and downs as and when they arrive. If you reach this transcendence level you will be living with Rule 7, Be Confident in your heart and mind, happy with what you do and confident this is the life you want to live. You will be giving yourself an excellent chance to be the person you want to be and to reach your deathbed fulfilled.

This is possible for any person with a free spirit, wanting to celebrate their uniqueness, who searches to find their own free identity and has a desire to be completely independent of others while fully respecting the difference of others and recognising every human being has a unique soul and the beauty of life is that we are all different. So, search for your uniqueness and celebrate your difference, no matter what level of society you are in. Happiness and unhappiness happen at all levels. People can transcend in life with little in the way of possessions and money but can meet all of Maslow's needs from what surrounds them. The key here is they are not materialistic or striving to be a billionaire: they simply love life and everything around them. That happiness comes primarily from their own contentment with who they are, and is enhanced by family and friends around them and the community they live in. However, people can also start life with little or nothing, and expect everything to be given to them. You will stay where you are if you don't try. Yes, in a caring society, there will be support for those unfortunate in life, but you still need to grasp the idea that it is *you* who will give you the life you want. Take responsibility for what you do and who you want to become. Look at the many successful people today who started with nothing. Look at the people who lost everything and then rebooted their lives. They are where they are today because they never stopped growing, they never stopped learning and they never stopped believing in achieving a good life. They took responsibility for themselves, controlled the emotion around who they are and what they do, and created a clear pathway in life by creating meaning across everything they do.

On the other hand, some people want for nothing and have all the money in the world, but are lonely, unhappy and feel vulnerable. They have taken responsibility to grow materialistically and greedily, seeking possessions and power at all costs. But they have missed out on love and belonging by using people and even climbing the social ladder on the backs of others.

Then there are those wealthy people have everything but stay grounded in life having achieved their success with humility, kindness and a desire to help others less fortunate than themselves. Philanthropy and kindness are powerful motivators for such people when they find themselves living a good life and can now share it with others.

What I want you to consider here is this: it doesn't matter where you are in life or what kind of life you lead now, you can transcend beyond self-actualization and become enlightened within yourself. But to do this you need to fulfil all your needs, take personal responsibility for all of them, make sure you strive to be the best you can be, and work with others in a constructively positive way to do this. Then you will become responsible for getting the best out of yourself, and from there your potential has no boundaries.

All these needs of Maslow's hierarchy, it is taking responsibility for all of them that is the key. This is achieved by taking control of your mind and building habits and behaviours that stay with you. Once you recognise the importance of self-responsibility at every level of your life, you stand a better chance of having a good life.

WARNING:

You must keep on top of each level of need and never get complacent about your state of mind or you can lose the good life, as I did. The good news is, the earlier in life you cotton on to the importance of each level of need being satisfied, the earlier you can enjoy the good life.

The Wheel of a Balanced Life: another useful model

The Wheel of a Balanced Life is a tool you can use to help you live a good life. You can only really reduce your risks in life if you address all parts of your life. Having a balanced life has so many benefits, particularly if you want to have some control over your basic needs and set a solid foundation for your future development. Those wanting to truly succeed and maintain enjoyment while doing so, recognise that a balanced life is essential. The Wheel of a Balanced Life complements Maslow's hierarchy of needs, particularly the basic needs such as physiological, safety, love and belonging. The twelve segments in the Wheel of a Balanced Life cover all the areas you need to consider if you strive to live a good life.

This simple exercise allows you to look at your life balance in an honest and safe way. It is your personal assessment of how you are doing in each area. The areas covered are: family life, social activity, career and vocation, self-development, attitude to life, health and fitness, financial security, home and work environment, travel and adventure, creative time, spirituality and personal relationships.

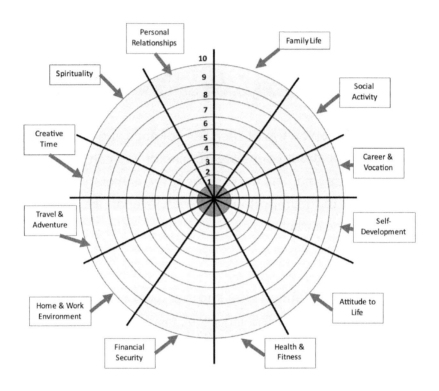

The Wheel of a Balanced Life

For this exercise, look at one of the twelve principles of the Wheel of a Balanced Life in isolation and mark yourself with a score from one to ten. Ten is the highest score you can give yourself: that being you are currently very happy and fulfilled, working at your best within that area. A score of one indicates you are very unhappy and have lost yourself within that area. If you mark one in any area you must look into it as a matter of urgency and reflect on how you will improve that score.

So, scale your feelings from 1 to 10. The key point here is you must be honest with yourself. No wilful lying or pretending that your reality is different. Control your emotions (which I will cover in detail in Rule 2) around what you are thinking and mark it in the moment you assess that area. By doing this, you can create and consolidate an authentic plan and solution for improving a poor score or maintaining a high score. You will give each element clear direction by the creation of meaning within each area. The aim is to make your life safer and happier. From this will come more security and more success in life.

Here is an overview of each area for you to mark 1 to 10:

Family Life

Family life is fundamentally important to your stability, so reflect upon your relationships with your partner, parents and children. *Hint*: you could break this area into those three separate elements. If you don't have immediate family, consider other support systems: how is your relationship with your alternative family?

To give you an example and to help you think about your situation, I will reflect on my family life. I have had a nuclear family of mum, dad and brother since birth. I have always known how lucky I am to have that foundation, but I know many people reading this may not be so fortunate. Regarding other family relationships, I haven't been so lucky. I'm not having a go at my past partners but more my ability to deal with a close relationship outside my direct family. So, regarding my direct family, my score would fluctuate between 7 and 10. As for my personal relationships, this has fluctuated from 1 to 10. This is the same with my children. The point I want you to think about here is that your score is *your* score. Yes, it may be difficult to deal with, or you may be lucky and be content. But remember, within you are Yin and Yang, and from chaos can come order. I would say this happened to me as I grew older, wiser and more mature. But remember too that from order can come chaos. The key point is to be honest with yourself and control your emotion when you are giving yourself a mark. Then take responsibility for where you are currently and create meaning around family relationships; even to the extent that you stay in or leave a relationship. You risk losing your good life if you begin to take your situation for granted, especially if you take the people close to you for granted.

WARNING

Never take anyone for granted, particularly if you have a soulmate and best friend for your partner, and you won't go far wrong. Start getting complacent, take your mind and heart out of the relationship, and things can and will go from good to bad.

So, scale your feelings from 1 to 10. The key point here is you must be honest with yourself. Control your emotion around what you are thinking and mark it in the moment you assess this area.

Social activity

Apply the same honesty as you reflect on your social life and how strong or weak it is. Is your social standing within your group solid and respectful, or distant and toxic? Think about the groups you are in and the friends you have. If you like solitude, take that into account as your circle will be smaller but possibly more genuine and authentic.

Grade your feelings from 1 to 10. No wilful lying or pretending that your reality is different. Mark it immediately: don't overthink it.

Career and vocation

Now reflect on your career, business or job. Are you happy in your career, or are you stuck in a rut? Is your job something you enjoy doing, or does it just pay the bills for now? Can you see yourself growing, progressing and excelling in that role? If you have a business, is it thriving or stagnating? Do you love what you do, or do you struggle getting up each day to go to work?

Again, scale your feelings from 1 to 10.

Self-development

My **Rule 4 to a Good Life is** keep learning. This is a non-negotiable rule. In any relationship or career, if you do not keep learning, complacency can be a killer and you will drift in life. So, think honestly: do you take self-development seriously or are you relying on what you know and do now? How much time do you set aside to learn new things, and are you experiencing new things? Do you actively educate yourself by reading, listening to or watching new and interesting material? How many seminars, shows, performances, events do you attend yearly? Do you actively seek to learn from others? Learning does not only mean going to school, college or university. Learning can be absorbed any time and from anywhere; for example, you can learn how to become a better mother, father, husband, wife, son or daughter. Learn how to become a better golfer, squash player, cook, traveller or DIY expert. Whatever you do, get better at it. Never stop self-developing and learning how to become the best you.

Mark your feelings from 1 to 10. Be honest with yourself and control your emotion around what you are thinking.

Attitude to life

What is your current attitude to life: are you an optimist, realist or pessimist? When you have setbacks do you dwell on them and feel sorry for yourself, or do you dust yourself down and go again? Lucky for me, I have dust-yourself-down-and-go-again as an inherent behaviour. You only get one go at this life, so make sure you give it the best you can. Always remember: the only thing you cannot buy is time and, once that is gone, it is gone. Do you look to blame others or take responsibility for all you do?

TOP TIP:
Take responsibility for your actions.
Enjoy what you do and actively seek new
challenges and experiences. Crack on with your
life with a smile. You will not regret it.
(Rule 1 to a Good Life)

I know people who have had some unlucky calls in life, but it is how you deal with those calls that develops the real you. It is your attitude that supports you in time of need. Remember each low period in life is actually a gift to improve yourself and learn. I lost my wife, Nicky, in 2016 through cancer. She was only forty-six when she died. The profound words she left me I will repeat again here, because they will stay with me for ever.

'When I die don't let two people die. I will be dead, but you are not. Please don't die mentally. Live your life to the full for me, but more importantly for yourself, and enjoy every day with a smile.'

She then said with her own cheeky smile, 'I will be checking on you and I'll haunt you if you don't.' Three days later, she passed away with me holding her hand. What an attitude to life my gorgeous wife Nicky had.

So please now, scale your feelings from 1 to 10. The key point here is you must be honest with yourself and no wilful lying. So, control your emotion around what you are thinking, and mark it in the moment you assess this area.

Health and fitness

How would you rate your health, given your age and physical conditions? Do you have a healthy diet and do you exercise regularly? Or are you a couch potato and avoid exercise in all its forms? This is critical to your overall well-being so please do not ignore it. Do not wait until a doctor says to you, 'I am sorry but you have…' Be proactive with your health and fitness. Don't ignore your mental well-being. You can spend hours exercising your body, and your brain is no different: make sure you exercise that too.

Grade your true feelings from 1 to 10. The key point once again is you must be honest with yourself, so no pretending that your reality is different.

Financial security

Where are you with your financial situation? Are you solvent or in debt? Are you good with money or not? Do you save or spend? Do you live within your means or do you overspend the money that comes in to you each month?

Again, scale your feelings from 1 to 10. Be honest with yourself, control your emotion around what you are thinking, and mark it in the moment you assess this area.

Home and work environment

This is about the quality of your home, your car, your office and the general spaces where you spend your time during the day and night, including time spent travelling. Are you happy with your car, house, gadgets, home comforts etc?

Award this area of life a score from 1 to 10. Be honest, and don't overthink it.

Travel and adventure

How much time do you give to travel? Do you get to experience other parts of the world (or even your own country)? Do you open yourself up to new experiences and adventures? Or do you go to the same places time and time again? Are you a home bird or an adventurer?

Scale your feelings from 1 to 10. Be honest with yourself.

Creative time

This one is about developing the right side of your brain, the Yang, or, as Professor Steve Peters would say, your chimp. Do you paint, write, play music or engage in other activities that channel your creativity? Or are you more of a consumer than a creator?

So please now, scale your feelings from 1 to 10. The key point here is you must be honest with yourself and no wilful lying or pretending that your reality is different. So, control your emotion around what you are thinking, and mark it in the moment you assess this area.

Spirituality

How much time do you devote to spiritual, meditative or contemplative practices that keep you feeling connected, balanced and peaceful? I am not just talking about religion or spirituality here. Do you practice mindfulness? Do you give yourself time for your mind to rest and think?

Grade your feelings from 1 to 10.

Personal relationships

You may be thinking that this is similar to Family Life. But this is not about the family group. This is about your one-to-one personal relationships. How happy you are within your current relationship? Maybe you can look at your platonic relationships and your emotional and physical relationships in two separate areas. Please recognise this last area is not easy to mark. You might be in Utopia and madly happy, or you may be suffering from toxicity and abuse. Recognise that, to live a good life, you must deal with the situation you are in right now, and personal relationships can be the hardest area of the Wheel of Life to deal with. So finally, scale your feelings from 1 to 10. The key point once again is you must be honest and no wilful lying to yourself or pretending that your reality is different. So, control your emotion around what you are thinking, and mark it in the moment you assess this area.

I have attached my results on the diagram below as an example. Time to do yours. Good luck and be brave.

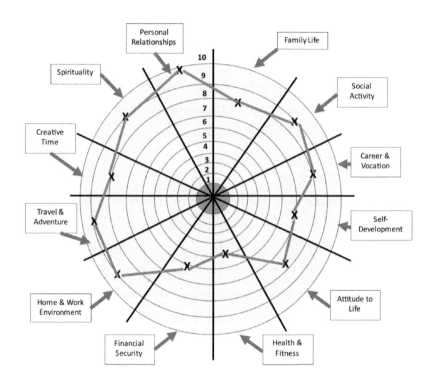

My example of the Wheel of a Balanced Life

How to improve your scores

Now reflect upon your scores and create solutions for improvement in all the areas that need it. Once you have been through all the areas, you will have a series of scores from one to ten. Doing this exercise, you will receive your own agency moments. Study the information you see across the lines you have created and you will start feeling the agency within your mind. Don't forget to control your emotions (Rule 2) by ensuring what you rely on mentally is authentic and honest; and create meaning (Rule 3) by giving yourself direction with an achievable goal for each area. You can now make choices and take agency in each area regarding what actions, in which order, you want to put in place to address each one; especially if you have some low scores.

Look at your low scores. Identify those areas that you need to focus on. Then create a plan to address the lower scores and work towards making them a score of ten. Remember: you are where you are, so keep learning, build on good habits and develop new behaviours. Enjoy what you do and be positive in your future direction. The power is now with you.

TOP TIP:
What you have been feeling, and now see graphically, will not go away until you address it, and until then there is a risk you will begin to drift in life. Take responsibility for your present, and your future will look after itself.
(Rule 1 to a Good Life)

Rule 1: Good Life Challenge

a. Take responsibility for everything you do in life from now on.

b. Take responsibility for your day-to-day activities and thoughts.

c. Take responsibility to change your life to better your happiness.

d. Take responsibility for the consequences of your decisions.

e. Take responsibility for your continued growth and success.

Let these statements flow over you and be aware of your drift danger signs. Here are some emotions you may have: *depression, fear, powerlessness, greed, anger, arrogance, manipulativeness, distraction, complacency and inflated ego.*

And now face the challenge

My challenge to you is embrace Rule 1 *now*: take responsibility for yourself across all situations you find yourself in. Accept your responsibility and own it. Realise how good and wonderful self-responsibility is. Be happy and confident in your life and know that it is *you* who is responsible for you. Recognise that the power of leading a good life is within every moment, every new opportunity, and that every day is a new journey. Remember, it is your life and you are responsible for you and all your levels of needs. So, strive for contentment in your heart, mind and life.

I know finding yourself in a dark destructive mindset is hard to deal with, and maybe you can see no way out of the dark pit you feel you are in. But taking responsibility for your life in this environment has enormous long-term benefits. Even for the most hardened criminal or corrupt politician, there is always a chance to change and catch yourself on your life's negative curve to destruction. Start gaining in life by taking responsibility for who you are and for where you find yourself. By taking responsibility for a wayward life, you are unlocking your chance of a true good life.

So, grab your life now and take responsibility for it. Celebrate your difference and learn something new each day. Grab every opportunity to experience and celebrate life with gratitude. In a group, team, organisation or business, know that if each one of you embraces responsibility and fully recognises that working and growing together is far greater than working apart, then everything and anything is possible. Irrespective of your background, gender or the skills, knowledge and experience you have, it is simply about being the best you can be each day and with a smile. Be confident in being you and be happy to work in all the areas within your Wheel of a Balanced Life. Remember, it is all about simply being the best you can be each day to help you live a good life. Then your future is yours once and forever.

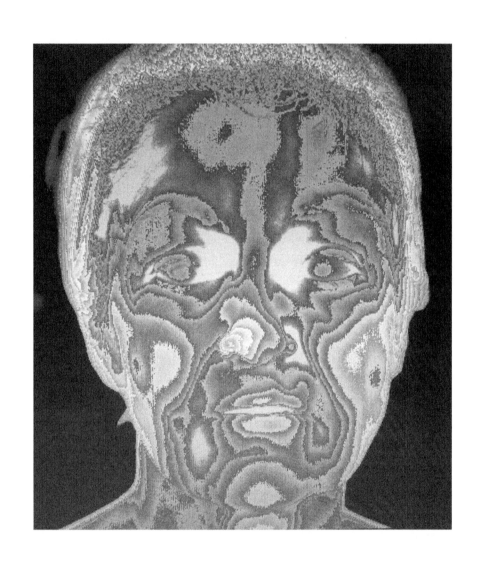

RULE 2
TO A GOOD LIFE:

CONTROL EMOTION

Why Do You Need to Control Your Emotions?

You cannot achieve anything with anger. When you get angry it comes from the agency you have received from a situation you have found yourself in or have walked into due to habit. Anger is merely a sign that you do not have the knowledge, skills or experience to deal with the situation; anger is the emotion that comes out. Really you are getting angry with yourself not the person you are with or the situation you are in. So, take agency and don't put yourself in those situations. Anger breeds more anger, so the chain must be broken by someone or something. You can achieve lots of great things with calmness and belief. The military special forces thrive on this factor. They know that letting anger get the better of them will cloud their judgement and could lead to their deaths.

Low altitude parachute drop.

Anger, calmness, doubt and belief live within the second stage of agency: the *feeling* of agency. Anger and doubt manifest when your neural system and brain battle the agency you have received through your senses. If you do not control that battle in the mind, then the mind will take control of you. There are imbalances, chemical and neurological, within the body that make the controlling of this battle even harder. But it is the complexity of your thoughts that can confuse and dictate your mental direction. Gossip, hearsay and tittle-tattle are toxic poisons that many fill their heads with. It amazes me that people will believe unjustified and unsubstantiated statements yet shy away from the truth. Belief in gossip and hearsay happens when people are mentally lazy. It is an easy get-out from thinking honestly, particularly to yourself. People will make any excuse without authentic reasoning. And, the dangers they cause are profound across that person's life. Many people in history have been victim to gossip-mongering: Aristotle, Seneca, Galileo, Darwin, even the great Einstein. In the modern day, we can look at Nelson Mandela, Florence Nightingale, Dr Martin Luther King and Alan Turing. All were subject to the manipulation of a prejudicial, unsubstantiated and uneducated narrative.

It is through controlling the accumulation of positive thoughts that we find the key to a smarter and better life. These negative or positive thoughts are formed in our minds as mental habits, and you know how hard it is to form a good habit or break a bad habit. Controlling the emotions around your weight, fitness, work ethic, business success, even the people around you, is essential to a smarter life.

Some struggle even to get out of bed in the morning to face the new day. Appreciate that, for some, through mental, medical or biological factors, getting out of bed is difficult, sometimes impossible to do. But the creation of a positive environment to help your team perform at the best of their ability together, cannot be achieved in a negative and destructive atmosphere. Therefore, recognise that, to improve across all the elements within your Wheel of a Balanced Life, thinking and reasoning in a constructively positive environment is the only way to live life smarter and lead a good life. This means allowing people to think, collect their thoughts and make decisions effectively in a balanced positive emotional state.

A fantastic book to carry out further reading in this area is *The Chimp Paradox: The Mind Management Programme for Confidence, Success and Happiness* by Professor Steve Peters. This book explains how the brain works psychologically and neurologically by discussing three areas: the computer, the human and the chimp. The computer is the process part of the brain, which is fed by the human and the chimp. The human is seen as the logical, structured area, the reality part of the brain. The chimp is the naughty trouble-maker, the adventurous and challenging area, the reactional, emotional part of the brain. The key to Peters' book is to recognise the role of the chimp and the human, and how they feed the computer part of your brain. It is the controlling of the emotional relationship between the two and the recognition of the strengths and weakness of both that help you through your life's journey to get the best out of your mindset.

Here is an example from my own life. My partner's son Matthew has Prader-Willi Syndrome[26]. This is an eating disorder that cannot be cured as it is a genetic condition caused by a deletion on chromosome 15. The saddest part of this syndrome is that the sufferer is never full and always hungry, always looking for food. Virtually every conversation is about food as the subject never leaves the sufferer's mind and their only goal in life is to eat. The most famous person I know of who has Prader-Willi Syndrome is Katie (Jordan) Price's son Harvey.

For us, cupboards need to be locked when not used, and money must be hidden so it cannot be stolen to get food. It feels like the sufferer is a predator for food and their desire for food takes up most of their thoughts throughout a day. Another feature of this horrible syndrome is that sufferers can be highly autistic and have a lower mental age range. For example, Matthew is thirty, but his functioning age has been assessed as six, and he looks and acts like a twelve-year-old. The magnificence and beauty of Matthew is that he always has a positive outlook: that is his gift to me and all around him. He has two rods in his back as a result of scoliosis so he has every excuse to be angry, and anyone who knows people with Prader-Willi Syndrome will know they do have big angry melt downs. From my perspective, Matthew is a bundle of positive fun who could justifiably be angry with life, but he isn't. That is partly down to his own attitude in life but more so to his mum's. Yes, she is strict with him, but he has exceeded his life expectancy of twenty years as he has been allowed to live a relatively normal life in which he is happy. Yes, he needs twenty-four-hour care, but his mum is consistently, constructively positive. She has an amazing trick she uses if he steals food, which happens on a daily basis: when she finds out, there are no consequences if he tells the truth. But there are punishments if he lies about it.

Perhaps not coincidentally, these are the foundation principles of a successful and effective company that adopts International Standards Organisation (ISO) standards[27] or Six Sigma techniques[28] and the like. These two standards create a framework of processes that recognise risks, deal with issues, and help maintain excellent standards, in a calm and collected way. These standards promote a culture of continuous self-development and advancement of individuals and excellence in the products or performances produced. Be honest about your risks, accidents and mistakes, then learning can take place. Lie about them and hide them, then a crisis is waiting around the corner, because you have put your life, work and business at risk. These standards encourage everyone to be their own 'point person' in life.

And this is how his mum helps Matthew control his emotions: by removing the anger from the situation and giving him tools to calm down. This allows him to have a think and then take agency of his own behaviour. His mum, Anna, has a fish tank, so he goes and talks to the tropical fish, or he will go and have a chat with Dora his greyhound, or he counts to ten. Generally, when we know Matthew has done something and we present it to him, he will say 'let me think about that' and he goes away and calms down. He always comes back and owns up to what he has done. By doing this, the risk is removed, his quality of life is improved, and his personal safety is maintained.

My *7 Rules to a Good Life* help you to simplify the process of achieving a good life, of living a safe, positive and productive life, a happy life: even for someone who has a condition like Matthew's. It makes sure you give yourself, or your team, the best chance of success in whatever you do, whether that is keeping fit, losing weight, running a successful business or being an elite athlete or entertainer. My *7 Rules* help you keep control of your emotions, no matter how hard that may be. If Matthew can do it, you have no excuse.

Keep a constructive and positive mindset

Maintaining a constructive, positive mindset is key to controlling your emotions. Rule 2 is about understanding and then managing *what* you think and *how* you think. Taking responsibility and controlling your emotions are the first steps to a good life. When you take responsibility for everything you do, remembering that some elements within your life may be harder than others to deal with, then you can lead yourself to a good life. But it is controlling the emotions around your acceptance of responsibility that makes it all work in a positive direction.

Me and my unit 847 during the Falklands War 1982

In 1982 I was a member of the UK task force to return the Falklands to British rule after the invasion by Argentinian forces. I served 847 Naval Air Commando Squadron: Wessex V Helicopters. Our unit coach, a lieutenant commander Special Boat Service, had a profound effect on me, on how I have led my life since and how I developed the first two elements of my *7 Rules*. He said in one of our coaching sessions on board the ship sailing towards our war destiny: 'in the theatre of war you will have a feeling you may die or are going to die. If you get angry then you will die. Give yourself a chance of not dying by staying as calm as you can. Control your fears and anger, be honest with yourself, accept the situation you are in, good or bad, and try to see a way out. If you become angry, there *is* no way out and you *will* die, so control your emotions at all times, and give yourself a chance to live.' This is why these elite forces are so professional in what they do: they acknowledge the dangers of uncontrolled anger, so they train their brains to manage it. Just like Matthew's mum does with him.

The wonderful vehicles of our unit, the
Wessex V Helicopters — 1982

When all individuals in the group have emotional control, anything is possible. Some readers may be thinking this is robotic, but I draw your attention to **Rule 7: Be Confident** and Enjoy What You Do. There is no point to living a smarter life and a good life if you're not enjoying it and you are not happy with what you're doing.

So how do you control your emotions?

Intellectual Intelligence, Emotional Intelligence and Spiritual Intelligence: How They Work Together

Many people have heard of intellectual intelligence (IQ) and emotional intelligence (EQ), but little is known of spiritual intelligence (SQ). Developing and working on your level of spiritual intelligence will help you live a smarter life and a good life. But this can only be achieved if you continually work on developing your intellectual intelligence (IQ) and emotional intelligence (EQ).

Spiritual intelligence

This involves the whole brain and is the driver of your overall intelligence. Spiritual intelligence synchronises processes within the whole brain by bringing together and harmonising the intellectual (left brain) and emotional (right brain) parts of the brain. Spiritual intelligence is linked to enlightenment and is seen as the higher dimension of brain. This is the ultimate level of peak performance when you are calm and happy. You are enjoying it while feeding the position of enlightenment. Feeling that you are taking responsibility for yourself and being authentic to yourself is the key to developing your spiritual intelligence through emotional control of the brain. So, your level of intelligence is fed by what you do and how you think about it. That is why it is fundamentally important to feed your brain through the experiences you allow yourself, and to manage your emotions with constructively positive thoughts, accurate, truthful data and information. Critical thinking, or Stoic thinking, is key to a higher form of intelligence. You give yourself the best chance in life with an informed decision-making framework within the agency process discussed earlier. When you take agency, you are able to make positive choices and take constructive actions.

Your intelligence is driven by the experiences you expose yourself to (receiving agency through your senses), the responsibility you place on those experiences, and by how you think and how you control your emotions. Therefore, the benefits to you of leading a smarter life and a good life come from the level and quality of the spiritual intelligence you generate. This can manifest itself through the growth of your wisdom, compassion, integrity, joy, love, creativity and inner peace. Enlightenment is a life goal many people strive for and is the ultimate goal regarding spiritual intelligence. Spiritual intelligence results in a sense of deeper meaning and purpose, combined with improvements in a wide range of important life and work skills.

How do you form and grow your spiritual intelligence?

There are two elements that feed the quality of your spiritual intelligence: intellectual and emotional intelligence. You may know *intellectual intelligence* as IQ or Intelligence Quotient. Your IQ level dictates your ability to problem-solve and embrace continuous learning across all parts of your life. From that continuous learning habit, you grow a high retention rate for skills and knowledge, as you question and practise skills in a positive and effective way.

Bruce Lee[29] once said, 'I am not fearful of the person who throws a thousand punches, but I am fearful of the person who throws the punch that they have practised a thousand times.' That is what elite athletes and performers do: they practise, practise, practise and then practise some more. They develop towards spiritual intelligence through continual practice and learning with their intellectual intelligence.

Jonny Wilkinson[30], the England rugby player, had one moment to win the Rugby World Cup Final in 2003. His drop goal gave England World Cup glory. He did this by developing his intellectual and emotional intelligence well before that kick; by practising and visualising such a kick over and over again. When that moment came, he took the responsibility and controlled his emotions to stay calm and execute the kick that he had done a thousand times before. It was just another kick in his mind. In that moment and that situation, many people would have crumbled. Jonny Wilkinson didn't: he had developed spiritual intelligence based on a foundation of intellectual and emotional intelligence. A great book to read that goes into the detail of this is called *The Pressure Principle: Handle Stress, Harness Energy, and Perform When It Counts* by Dr Dave Alred MBE[31].

To get to a level of spiritual intelligence, you must embrace the idea that life is an organic sea of changes and that, on occasions, you will need to modify and review what you do and how you do it. Critical thinking about and continual practice of what you do, as well as possessing a continuous learning habit, ensure you give yourself the best chance to achieve the best possible performance in everything you do, whether that be for yourself in life, in relationships, working in a team, running a business or becoming an elite human being in your chosen field.

Intellectual intelligence, known as IQ, is the cognitive (thinking) activity involved in perception and storing and recalling memory, that leads to reasoning and resolving problems. Emotional intelligence, known as EQ, complements and harmonises intellectual intelligence. This is about taking responsibility for yourself, being aware of who you are authentically; having the ability to self-regulate, be self-disciplined and moderate how you behave in any given situation. It's about being self-motivated to achieve your best while having empathy for others, knowing you are unique but so is everyone else. From this, you should be able to feel the link to intellectual capital and understand how having a social connection to the people around you are also key to your emotional intelligence. Simply, this is the ability to understand, use and manage your own emotions in positive ways to relieve stress, communicate effectively, empathise with others, overcome challenges and defuse anger and conflict. Remember that anger is the most destructive of emotions and nothing good can come of it.

"Anybody can become angry — that is easy. But to be angry with the right person and to the right degree and at the right time and for the right purpose, and in the right way — that is not within everybody's power and is not easy."

—Aristotle

Spiritual intelligence lies within the world of wisdom which is a key part of our friend Aristotle's work.

There has been an argument resonating about which is the greater, IQ or EQ. To me, that seems a bit weird as to have both and work on both are equally important. To strive towards a good life, work on both intelligences effectively to become wise; this in itself will help you get the best out of both sides of your brain, the analytical left side and the creative right side. It is known that when someone has high levels of IQ and EQ then anything is possible, but as a minimum you can give yourself a better chance of success, allowing yourself to live the best life you can. It also feeds into your self-confidence and your ability to achieve your goals.

This has been Daniel Goleman's[32] life's work. He is an author, psychologist and science journalist, his passion being brain and behaviour sciences. His 1995 book *Emotional Intelligence: Why It Can Matter More Than IQ* is a great read, a first port of call for further reading. However, there are many other amazing people out there who I do not cover in this book, but who you can tap into to build your own knowledge around this subject. Please read the *Bibliography and Notes* at the end of this book and use them as a springboard for your own independent research.

THINK OF THIS:
On an individual basis, having intellectual and emotional intelligence is one thing, but the power of having a team or an organisation with both IQ and EQ would be something special. Think about what you could achieve together with team spiritual intelligence. Now that would be amazing.

Let us take that up another level and think about what we could be capable of if the entire human race could achieve spiritual intelligence together. You may be thinking this is impossible, but I will never say that: I am a natural optimist. If you think it is impossible and come up with every excuse for it to stay impossible, it will be impossible. We only need to find a way to change the narrative.

Yes, it is a bloody hard goal to achieve, but one thing Covid-19 has proven is that, if the world can get together to create vaccines so quickly when given a common goal to get rid of a pandemic, then the world has shown it is capable of achieving collective IQ and EQ to some degree. The Covid outbreak was declared a Public Health Emergency of International Concern on 30 January 2020 and a pandemic on 11 March 2020, and the global death count by 2023 stood at **6,866,434**. The Covid pandemic experience has shown that working together globally can have profound effects to achieve a greater good. Sadly, we can now see the world drift apart from the initial pandemic regarding working together, with focus now being transferred to more localised individual needs and requirements.

However global, known risks require a team effort to be resolved.

The existential threats of global warming and climate change will only be resolved if we as one planet work together once again. We know now what IQ and EQ are, so we only have ourselves to blame if we don't deal with climate change effectively. Sadly, humans react only when something goes drastically and tragically wrong or someone dies. With climate change, for many years now globally we have been in receipt of agency and we are currently, finally, in the process of a global feeling of agency: we need to be quick and start *taking* agency for a better future; together.

To recap thus far: to strive towards the good life and to live life smarter, get to know how your brain works in controlling your emotion and removing anger. Understand how you can build your intellectual and emotional capacity to become spiritually intelligent; you won't go far wrong in life if you do that. Being the best you can be each day, and enjoying it, will become a natural behaviour and habit within you and the people around you.

Twelve Life Principles That Drive Peak Performance

Here is another tool to help you with **Rule 2: Control Your Emotions.** Before we start setting out these principles, it is always useful to set a benchmark of outstanding role models or examples for ourselves. So, pick an inspiring person to give you an insight into what is possible. It might be Steve Jobs[33], founder of one of the peak-performing world companies, Apple. Or Elon Musk[34], highly successful entrepreneur and adventurer. Or Wayne Gretzky[35], who is arguably the greatest American hockey player ever. Or Jurgen Klopp[36] (Liverpool Football Club) or Alex Ferguson[37] (Manchester United Football Club) who are great English football league managers. It could be your father or mother, an old teacher, a good friend, a politician, sports person; in fact, it can be anyone who you know to excel at life and inspire you. But please choose wisely.

Common themes with people who are emotionally, intellectually and spiritually intelligent is consistency, integrity, honesty and a belief in living a good life. They appreciate that there are some key factors in life that you need to home in on to live the good life and strive for peak performance. They understand that having incremental small successes is the foundation of and makes great success possible. That is why it is important to take one day at a time, one match at a time, and one performance at time; being the best you can be. Having this incremental success mentality, you are compounding good habits and behaviours each day. That day then turns into a good week, then a good month, a good year and ultimately a good life. Practising and making perfect are essential ingredients of this, even if you do not succeed each time you try. Gretzky's famous saying encapsulates what peak performance is all about: 'You miss 100% of the shots you don't take'. If you don't have a go, you will never know what is possible and, if you never try, you will never get there. So, being positive is essential to forward success. Being focussed and having a desire to continually learn helps you not only stay ahead of your curve in life but gives you a better chance of finding out what could be achieved in the future with effort and discipline.

From that, you control your emotions by not getting too carried away with your successes and not getting too down in your not-so-good moments. Remember, life is full of peaks and troughs. Make sure you look forwards from so called failures and use all problems and obstacles as opportunities. Continually grow your knowledge base and experiences by expanding your horizons and seeing different worlds and cultures. Make sure you find the best teammates and partners by surrounding yourself with authentic, creative, positive people who hold similar values to you. Always push yourself in a healthy way through the risks you take, giving yourself effective challenges that push your boundaries. Taking responsibility for yourself and controlling your emotions create a foundation to live a good life by continually building your intellectual capacity and spiritual intelligence. You can do this in all parts of your life; so, choose your mentors and inspirational people wisely. Luckily for me, my early and life-long inspiration is my dad, with my grandad as my mentor.

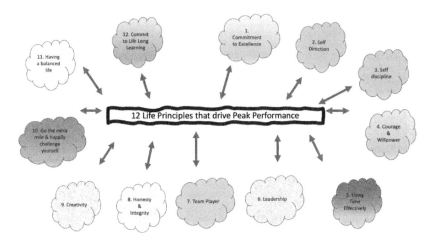

12 Life Principles that Drive Peak Performance

These 12 Life Principles that Drive Peak Performance give you some headings to work on to achieve a good life. This is an exercise you can use at any time, by assessing on a scale of 1 to 10 how good or bad you are in each area, 1 being the lowest and ten meaning you excel in that area. So, look at each of the 12 areas and think how it applies to you now. As with the Wheel of a Balanced Life exercise earlier, scale your feelings from 1 to 10. The key point once again is you must be honest with yourself: no wilful lying or pretending that your reality is different. So, control your emotion around what you are thinking as you assess and mark each area.

1. Commitment to excellence
2. Self-direction
3. Self-discipline
4. Courage and willpower
5. Using time effectively
6. Leadership
7. Team player
8. Honesty and integrity
9. Creativity
10. Going the extra mile and happily challenging yourself
11. Having a balanced life
12. Commitment to lifelong learning

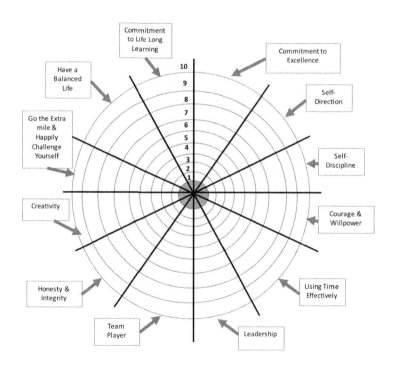

12 Life Principles that Drive Peak Performance exercise

How to improve your marks

Like with the Wheel of a Balanced Life, reflect upon the marks and create solutions for improvement in all areas that need it. Once you have worked through all the principles you will have a series of scores from one to ten. By doing the exercise you have given yourself agency. With the information you absorb, you will start feeling that agency. Do not forget to control your emotions and create meaning for each area. You can now make choices and take agency by deciding which actions in what order you put in place; especially if you have some low scores. Identify those areas that you need to focus on. Then create a plan to address the lower score and work towards a score of 10. Here is my example, and you can clearly see I need to work on my time management and balanced life style.

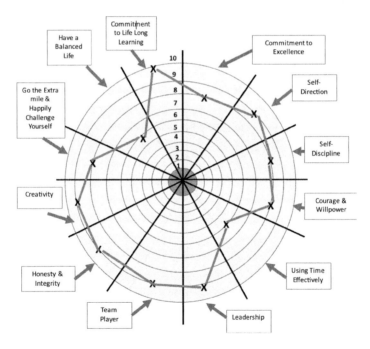

My example of 12 Life Principles that Drive Peak Performance

Remember: you are where you are, so keep learning to develop and strengthen new habits. Enjoy what you do and be positive in your future direction.

WARNING

Do not ignore this exercise. The danger is you may begin to drift in life because whatever negativity you feel now will not go away until you address it. So, take responsibility for your present and the future will look after itself. Good luck.

NB: My YouTube Channel Live Life Smarter Coaching Programme reflects the structure of this book breaking down each of the elements into concise coaching videos with key points, exercises, various models and theories.

https://www.youtube.com/@livelifesmartercoachingpro6615/
featured

How Do You Control Your Emotions?

You should now appreciate you control your emotions by having a level of spiritual intelligence, but you also need an understanding of your level of consciousness. David Hawkins[38] presents this eloquently in his book *Power vs Force: The Hidden Determinants of Human Behaviour.*

The graphic below illustrates how, in regard to controlling your emotions, having the power is greater than forcing the issue. People may shy away from the rawness of this theory and model as it highlights the prejudice in all its forms that we hold within ourselves. Humans have difficulty admitting when they are not good at something, but this is where most personal benefit is gained: when you accept in a positive way that you do not know or cannot do something. Prejudice is the prejudgement of others and events. When you hold prejudice for another, based on subjective, unsubstantiated evidence, you are forcing your brain to accept a position through anger, denial, fear, grief, guilt and shame (all negative behaviours). This is compounded when you make a judgement based on lack of knowledge, skills or experience: you will be in denial of one or more of these deficiencies. The hyperactivity of anger forces you to have *issues* in the mind. Before we cover power versus force, it may help to clarify what is a risk and what is an 'issue'.

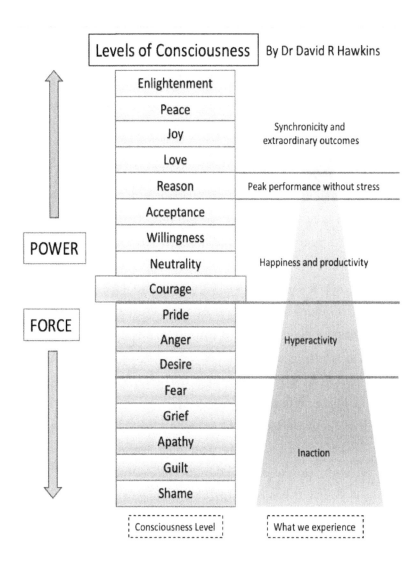

Levels of Consciousness | By Dr David R Hawkins

Consciousness Level	What we experience
Enlightenment	
Peace	
Joy	Synchronicity and extraordinary outcomes
Love	
Reason	Peak performance without stress
Acceptance	
Willingness	
Neutrality	Happiness and productivity
Courage	
Pride	
Anger	Hyperactivity
Desire	
Fear	
Grief	
Apathy	
Guilt	Inaction
Shame	

POWER

FORCE

Power versus Force diagram

What is the difference between an issue and a risk?

To help us understand what an issue in the mind is, it is helpful to compare it to what a risk is. Risks are feelings of uncertainty within your thought processes that expose you to a potential mistake or accident. They lie within the *'feeling of agency'* process as things *you think could happen* and therefore need consideration and thought. Nothing has actually happened: you just feel something could happen or something is wrong. This is what a risk is: something you think about and have thought towards. The *power* comes from dealing with the risk because you *want* to rather than because you have been *forced* into dealing with it. Take responsibility for your risks: *I feel I am getting depressed; I feel I am putting on weight, I feel I am spending too much, I feel my performance is dropping...* The risk you feel needs to be assessed, thought through and dealt with now; otherwise, it will become an *issue*.

An issue is when something *has happened* and needs urgent consideration in the moment of discovery. An issue is an immediate physical or practical experience that has an emotional effect on you now. *I am depressed; I am putting on weight, I am spending too much, my performance is dropping...* An issue therefore derives from a risk ignored. A risk *might happen*; an issue *has happened*.

Don't lose focus on **Rule 2: Controlling Your Emotion:** optimise learning towards living a good life. You must deal with both risks and issues before they compound and develop into something else.

So, allow your left brain to start to challenge you right brain and vice versa. The negative trajectory of the mind can lead to all sorts of destructive emotions. Sadly, it is only when a catastrophic event occurs, usually ending in injury or death, that the penny drops and things change in a more constructive way. For example, a person might be diagnosed with cancer and have only three months to live. They know they let the signs go ignored, through fear and anger. Fear and anger have forced them to make the decision to ignore the signs. If you are in a toxic, unhealthy relationship, you might force your own inaction through feelings of guilt or shame. It is the same with bullying and hatred. When you are angry with someone, it is you who has placed yourself in that position of anger, not them. The first rule of risk assessment is remove yourself from the risk, and do not let it become an issue. Give yourself the power to deal with things mentally: do not allow them to be forced upon you.

Anger has similar elements to failure. Think of this: failure does not exist. (I will explain this in more detail later in the book.) When I joined the Royal Navy in 1979, I was given this wise advice by my trainers and it has been embedded within me since. So, when I do something wrong or not so well and do not achieve what I want, I have not failed. My trainers explained that this is only a moment within my experience where it is time to look at myself. Take responsibility for the moment you are in and give yourself the power to deal with it. Stay calm, control your emotions and accept and reflect that you have not failed, so do not get angry. Accept that in that moment you lacked knowledge, skills or experience to deal with what was happening around you. So, take responsibility for your situation, control your emotion and remember **Rule 4: Keep Learning**. When you get to this point you give yourself the power to move forward through neutrality, willingness and acceptance to deal with the situation. You give yourself the power of reason by accepting that you need further development and growth within that experience. The icing on the cake, in regard to giving yourself the power, is that, if you control the emotion and reaffirm a positive trajectory in life, you will be happy, peaceful and joyful that you have reached an opportunity for advancement in life.

One of the most emotionally intelligent events I have been fortunate to observe is the military incident command licensing process in 1995. It was something I tried to introduce in 1996 to the fire service with the support of my mentor and senior fire training officer Mike Bitcon who ended up being the Chief Fire Officer of Fife Fire

Service in Scotland but passed away sadly from the horrible illness Motor Neurone Disease. To Mike, and his wife Gill, I will be eternally indebted for believing in me. As part of that development and research of command skills in the nineties, I had unique access to observe and research the military licensing process for all commanders in the military, mainly around bomb disposal of EODs and IEDs. In the military you cannot take charge of a command position (in charge of an event or incident) if you have not been through a rigorous licensing process to see if you have the right knowledge, skills and, more importantly, the emotional ability and stability to take charge of a major incident. It takes a unique human with high emotional, intellectual and spiritual intelligence to take charge of a major incident. Command licences needed to be renewed at least once a year to ensure each commander was still the right person to hold this role. I was therefore lucky to observe many of these licensing events. One assessment I observed was of a senior commodore who was due to be transferred abroad. A major part of the commodore role was incident commander. To run incidents, an officer had to be licensed either six-monthly or annually. This was dependent on the severity of risk they could potentially attend. Each incident commander was assessed across a series of real-life exercises for command skills and knowledge. In addition, candidates went through an assessment of mental discipline and behavioural control. On this occasion, the candidate facing the scenario was already on a final red warning as he had made critical mistakes on previous exercises; another critical mistake would mean he would not get his command licence and, therefore, could not hold the role of incident commander. And, if he failed two licence assessments, he would be deemed not able to take charge of incidents thereafter as a miliary incident commander. The scenario that faced the candidate was to attend an air dropped bomb (EOD) that had been found in a hut on top of a hill. The bomb lay close to a small village and major power lines. I will not go into too much detail of the assessment process, but the first part is called a 'long recce' from a distance, leading ultimately to a 'close-in recce'. You may have seen this when a bomb disposal expert in a green suit goes close up to attend a bomb. This is done if a long recce does not give the commanding officer enough information on how to assess the incident to set their 'positive action'. Positive action is when all the decision-making elements have been gathered and it is time to take a decision. So, the commanding officer is happy with the bomb they have, they know the steps to take and how to 'low order' the bomb or diffuse it. Low order is when bomb teams use a technique to decommission a bomb by using explosives or impinging jets, in the hope that the known ordinance device reacts like a giant sparkler with no destructive blast. When the experts are given confirmation from the off-site team that the positive action they have designed is agreed, they go in and carry out the agreed action. Obviously, there is no guarantee the device will not 'high order', which is when a bomb is detonated and there is a destructive blast.

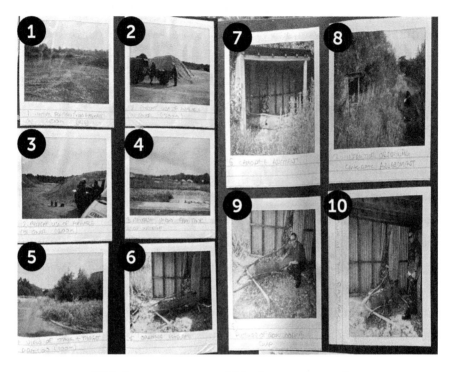

This is a sequence of 10 photos show the
assessment of an ordnance licensing process.

So, the candidate gathered all the information, sent what he knew
to the off-site team, and was given the green light to action his attempt
to defuse the bomb. He carried out the agreed defusing technique.
The assessors asked the candidate if he was happy with what he had
done and if the bomb was safely defused in his mind. The candidate
confirmed that the actions he had carried out had disarmed the bomb.
He was then asked by the assessor, 'What happens now?' So, he
requested a low-loader lorry for the bomb to be taken off site. Finally,
he had to say, 'End of exercise' as he deemed the scene safe. The assessor gathered the comments and marks for decisions to be taken by the
whole assessment team on the candidate's performance and whether or

not they would issue a command licence. The candidate looked quite happy once the debrief began as he hit all the early marks. But I saw him completely wilt when the assessor presented the side detonator on the bomb, that he had missed. If he had moved the bomb onto the low-loader and it had travelled through the village, the bomb would have gone off, causing a major incident with the potential for large loss of life. Plus, the major power lines would have gone down and stopped electricity to the surrounding communities. The outcome was he was issued a final red mark, was not allowed to go on draft to the overseas role and was barred from managing any future incidents as an incident commander.

You may be thinking: where does control of emotion come in for this candidate, a senior military officer who could no longer manage and lead incidents? The emotional control came in his reaction in an interview he kindly allowed me to conduct after he received the result of the assessment. I asked him how he felt about no longer being allowed to lead incidents as a commander. His reply was, 'yes, it is a tough thing to take but really I have to accept the results because, over two attempts, I made potentially fatal mistakes that could have caused a large loss of life.' He continued: 'therefore I need to look at other avenues and roles for my career as I lack the judgement and required behaviours to manage and lead an ordnance incident safely.' I asked him how he felt about being assessed by low-ranking officers and about the assessment process itself. His reply was, 'not a problem as the assessor is chosen for being the best of the best'. He continued, 'I have been across twelve independent assessments over two attempts. They have authentically assessed me correctly. I now have to deal with that. As for their rank, that doesn't come into it. It is the quality, skillset and experience they have that matters, and they are definitely the right people to be doing this.' Here was a high degree of emotional intelligence displayed by an officer who accepted he was not the right person to do this job even though it had been his career goal and desire. He accepted the outcome, rather than kid himself or blame another reason for his unsuccessful attempt at the tests.

WARNING

Humans don't like to be wrong or found to be incapable of doing something. You will know or feel if you are out of your depth or out of your comfort zone. Accepting you have reached your skill, knowledge or experience limits is a tough call, but take responsibility for that. You may need to either go again in the learning journey or accept this is not for you.

This incident was my catalyst to assess the value of licensed and unlicensed incident commanders for my PhD, which was entitled: 'It is the wrong time to learn your command skills at the incident scene.' Happily, the military have realistic assessments in place to prevent this being the case. The emergency services still have a lot to do in this area of work at senior levels. I will leave that with you.

Another method of emotional control is through audits. I used to do audits at all levels in the emergency services, business and education. I am confounded why people and organisations see audits and questions about work practice in a negative way. True learning only takes place from a position of unknowing and with some vulnerability. Learning does not come from what you do well or correctly; it comes when you are alive to the things that do not go as you expect: mistakes, accidents and unexpected experiences. So do not see these events as failures or negatives; see them as gifts to help you improve, grow and develop. Take responsibility for what you are doing and the situation you are in, control your emotion and change the narrative from a negative position to a positive one.

I know when I first heard about this, it took me some time, in fact many years, to accept it and see the behaviours required. I could not get my head around it at all. I was forcing my thoughts through fear, in an uncontrolled and non-evidence-based way, as I lacked the skills, knowledge and experience to assess what was going on. Trust me, if you can get your head around how to control your emotions while taking responsibility for yourself, your opportunities to grow, learn, develop and enjoy experiences will go through the roof, even to the stage that you can become self-enlightened. Not many reach that calm, pure, conscious state, but it is available to everyone and anyone. You only need to let it grow organically through the powers you give yourself, through controlling your emotions rather than forcing the situations on yourself.

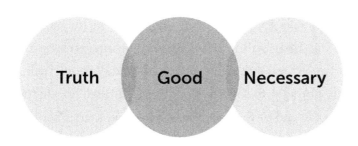

Socrates' Three Sieves

To end this chapter on **Rule 2: Control Emotion**, I would like to introduce you to Socrates' Three Sieves, the three filter questions you should ask yourself when you are assessing information you are about to share. Unjustified and unsubstantiated gossip or opinion is a danger in society. The cumulative effect of untruth on others is something you can reflect upon and deal with on a personal level. Once it starts, untruth can become a virus in society that can cause unnecessary and untold damage. When, and if, the truth is finally known, the stupidity of the original unjustified and unsubstantiated falsehoods can be seen by all. Why not search for the truth first? To do this, you can use Socrates' three sieves.

The sieve of truth

Question: Are you sure what you are going to say or share is true?

Have you heard it yourself or watched it with your own eyes? Have you the raw evidence that it is true? If you overheard it through gossip, hearsay or tittle-tattle, then you have failed the first sieve (question). You cannot be certain of its truth. If you have doubt, open your gateway to learning (**Rule 4 to a Good Life: keep learning**).

Do you remember the game in school, Pass the Message? So, you all line up and someone whispers a paragraph into the first person's ear, let's say 'Sally sells sea shells on the sea shore.' As the message passes down the line there will be dilution and misinterpretation because, although you ask each time 'have you got that?', people will say 'yes' even when they have misheard the message through one distraction or another. At the end of the line, the original message is spoken out by the last person and comes out as 'Peter Piper picked a peck of pickled peppers.' So, when you *believe* something to be the truth, *make sure* it is the truth. Once a lie or twist on information spreads, it compounds until checked or stopped.

If the test of the first sieve is not successful, present the second sieve.

The sieve of goodness

Question: Will you tell me something good or positive about this person or thing?

If you were going to say bad things about the person, you have failed the second sieve (question). Why talk or think about someone in bad terms? Remember, nothing good can be achieved from a negative position. Anger, jealousy and hatred do not achieve anything: even with your worst enemy. When there is a negative atmosphere or environment it can only be changed by building good. Think about conflicts in the past. They have all at some point ended up with talking to find common ground. So, control your emotions and do not be destructive in your thoughts. **My Rule 5 to a Good Life: Compounding Decisions**, and **Rule 6: Working Together,** will highlight the reasons for this and give you some tools to help you develop in a positive direction.

If you do not pass the second sieve, look at the third sieve.

The sieve of what is necessary

Question: Is it necessary to tell me what you are so excited about?

Generally, it is not necessary to comment if you are excited about something that is destructive and untrue. Socrates says if the story you are about to tell me is not true, good or necessary, forget it and do not bother me with it. So, think about what you say before you say it and filter it through the three sieves of Socrates.

The same sieves can be applied not only to words but also to a toxic destructive atmosphere. When you see injustice or hurt, apply the three sieves and they will address the issue to move towards a positive trajectory. Now that is real control of your emotions, and the benefits for you and people around you are enormous for living a good life.

Controlling emotion is about being in the moment, making sure that the moment feels right and that you are happy with how you feel. Controlling your emotion in the moment is about believing in that moment for good rather than bad. So, make sure you control how you think and make sure you banish wilful lies from your mind. Use Socrates' three sieves to help you do that effectively each day.

Salem Witches

Here is a powerful story about receiving agency through misinformation, about the feeling of agency when that misinformation lands in our minds and we begin to process it. If we do not control our mental filters, we can be easily manipulated by others.

A friend told me about a powerful lesson in her daughter's school class. They're learning about the Salem Witch Trials, and their teacher told them they were going to play a game. "I will come around and whisper to each of you whether you're a witch or a regular person. Your goal is to build the largest group possible that does NOT have a witch in it. At the end, any group found to include a witch gets a failing grade."

The teens dove into grilling each other. One large group formed, but most of the students broke into small, exclusive groups, turning away anyone they thought gave off even a hint of guilt.

"Okay," the teacher said. "You've got your groups. Time to find out which ones fail. All witches, please raise your hands." No one raised a hand.

The kids were confused and told the teacher he'd messed up the game. "Did I? Was anyone in Salem an actual witch? Or did everyone simply believe what they'd been told?"

And that is how you teach kids how easy it is to divide a community. Shunning, scape-goating and dividing destroy far more than they protect.

(Origin Unknown)

Rule 2: Good Life Challenge

a. From this point forward lose anger in your life and control your emotions.

b. Control your emotions across all your day-to-day activities and thoughts.

c. Control your emotions and shift your mind's narrative away from a destructive perspective.

d. Keep controlling your emotions to grow and succeed.

e. Know that controlling your emotions will lead to your happiness.

Let these statements flow over you and look out for your drift danger signs. Emotions and feelings you may have:
Depression, fear, sense of no option, doubt, denial, anxiety, frustration, arrogance, distraction, anger, complacency and ego.

And now face the challenge!
Control your emotions primarily by removing anger from your mind whatever situation you are in. No matter how hard or difficult the situation may be, give yourself time out to connect with your mind and remove that feeling, knowing that nothing good can come from

anger. Recognise that a negative emotion is a signal that you are in a moment where you don't know something, don't have the skills to deal with it nor have an experience to call upon. So, change the narrative and strive to stay calm in your heart and mind. Build up your emotional and intellectual intelligence and feed you spiritual intelligence. Work on all your life principles and grow them each day. Don't allow risks to become issues. Recognise that what gives you greater control over your emotions is embedding good habits and behaviours into your day-to-day life, rather than forcing the issues. Think when you are about to share information with others: use the three sieves of Socrates before you do. If it is not true, not good or unnecessary, don't share it. Always remember anger is the great destructive force and will cause you to drift in life. Recognise that the power to lead a good life comes from controlling your emotions within every moment, every new opportunity and that every day is a new journey. YOU CAN DO IT! No matter how bad or fearful you may feel, if you look hard enough, there are always options, no matter how hard you think they may be. It is your life: you need only to change the narrative in your mind and control your wilful lies. *I am ugly* – NO, YOU ARE NOT! *I can't do this* – YES, YOU CAN! *There is no reason to live* – YES, THERE IS! So, stop creating false or misleading impressions now. Taking emotional control of a wayward life is the key that unlocks the true good life. With emotional control, grab every opportunity and celebrate the life around you.

If you are in a team, organisation or business and you have emotional control and respect for one another, recognise that working together and growing together, is far greater than working apart: which is explained in detail in my **Rule 6 Working Together.** Embrace difference and celebrate diversity, knowing this is about being the best you can be each day as a team.

Stay calm and be the best you can be each day and with a smile. If you grab your life now and take control of your emotions, you will never regret doing so and your future will be yours once and forever.

RULE 3
TO A GOOD LIFE:

CREATE MEANING

Why You Need to Create Meaning

You cannot achieve anything without giving it meaning. Everything in life should have meaning. Everything in life *needs* meaning: from getting up each morning to have a good day, running a family to give you a foundation in life, earning a wage to do the things you want in life, running a business because you want to bring something to the market, to becoming an elite athlete because you want to be a champion. You cannot do anything in life without meaning; even down to eating to support your bodily requirements and give you the fuel to live every day. If you do not eat, you die. If you eat too much, you get fat and, if you eat too little, you get weak. The desire for food, and its meaning for you, is your responsibility. Controlling your emotions around food will keep you at your optimum weight. So, clarifying your meaning in regard to food is essential for a healthy life. This then gives meaning and purpose to your responsibilities in life and helps you control your emotion. Now you will begin to see the critical links between my *7 Rules to a Good Life*; they complement and support one another. They are completely interchangeable.

So meaning is created and driven by setting goals. Your goals come from your dreams and thoughts. Dreams range from the simple to the audacious, but dreams need to be personal. You dream of buying that wedding dress. You dream of playing for Liverpool Football Club (sorry, I am biased here). You dream of running your own business, or you dream of having a family. Elon Musk dreams of interplanetary travel. Might seem crazy and outlandish to most, but it is his dream. Your dreams and thoughts must have meaning within your life for them to come alive, or they will stay merely dreams. Turning your dreams into reality is possible. Anything is possible: this is what drives the advancement of Earth and its civilisations. This is what drives who you are and what you want to be. And you are responsible for making it happen. Meaning gives you direction.

Think about this: if you want to go on holiday, you will think of what your ideal vacation looks like and dream about where it will take place; camping as a family, visiting Disney World in Florida, climbing Kilimanjaro. Your dreams are unique to you.

A great book I highly recommend is *Jeopardy: The Danger of Playing It Safe on the Path to Success* by Wilfred Emmanuel-Jones[39]. Wilfred was a black man in the heart of Birmingham, England, in a very poor environment. But he had a dream to be a farmer which was out of context with the area he was brought up. He was told that his dream was madness, impossible and ridiculous, even by his family. He would never be capable of it. But Wilfred achieved his dream and bought a 30-acre farm on the Devon/Cornwall border. At time of writing, it is reported his businesses are worth more than £322million. The barriers that were raised against Wilfred were many. The prejudice, stereotypical views and racism he faced never deterred him from his dream of having a farm. He gave meaning to his dreams and set himself goals as he went along. He took risk in his life, which he talks about as 'jeopardy' (recognising the role of risk), and embraced it at every step. Wilfred gave his life meaning, and you can do that too.

So have your dreams, whatever they are, but give them meaning in your life. Anchor your dreams with meaning through setting goals. If you want to lose weight, give it meaning, be that through an event, a sport or for basic health reasons. And anchor it by setting suitable but challenging goals. If you want to start a business, give it meaning and anchor it by setting goals and attaching timescales.

WARNING

Your dreams will not happen if you don't give them meaning. They will not happen if you doubt they will happen: fact. You cannot achieve anything with a negative or destructive trajectory. You will wilfully lie to yourself in order not to take responsibility for that meaning in your life. You will make every excuse that where you want to be is not important in your life. The most dangerous comment is 'this has nothing to do with me': yes, it bloody does. Being a bystander in life is *not* doing nothing: it is an acceptance that you are happy with the status quo. How do you think politicians get into power? They rely on the high percentage of people who say: 'I don't vote, I am not interested in politics.' When you do that, you give the status quo a vote.

So even by voting in an election, you give yourself meaning and not only yourself but your country too. If you don't, you can't blame anyone else if you are not happy with your government.

Please recognise that, when you do not give yourself meaning, you can and will drift in life. Do not let that happen. Acknowledge that you and only you are responsible for your life and the world directly around you, for good or bad.

If you give everything in your life meaning, everything and anything is possible. You will make your dreams and desires come alive: even the outlandish dreams of Elon Musk regarding interplanetary travel. You can live your dreams and live life smarter by giving those dreams meaning. You will not regret it.

How Do You Create Meaning?

Creation of meaning is essential as it is a direct statement of your investment in your life. Why would you not invest in yourself? It is said that John Lennon[40], a member of the band The Beatles from Liverpool, was asked as a child at school to write an essay:

"When I was 5 years old, my mother always told me that happiness was the key to life. When I went to school, they asked me what I wanted to be when I grew up. I wrote down 'happy'. They told me I didn't understand the assignment, and I told them they didn't understand life."

—John Lennon

This simple statement gave him meaning for all of his life. Always remember, the genius of living a good life is in the simplicity you place on your life. The difficulty is the understanding of the simplicity; the courage is actually keeping to those dreams; the challenge is living them authentically and honestly, and with a smile: my Rule 7.

You will invest in a house, you will invest in a car, so why not invest in your life? You invest in yourself by growing your personal philosophy of life, by having dreams and putting time and mental effort into those dreams, giving them meaning and thereafter setting goals to achieve them. Creation of meaning is the foundation to your forward trajectory in life.

WARNING

If you give yourself negative meaning through doubt, that negative meaning you place upon yourself will lead you to drift in life. So, create positive constructive meaning. Even if it is simply to get up in the morning, the creation of that constructive meaning allows you to form a critical pathway towards your goals.

Through meaning you can create your own critical path in life, the steps you need to take through the decision-making process. This is what cognitive behavioural therapists and personal counsellors do: they get you to form your own critical pathway from a bad, sad or confused place, by setting goals for yourself. The creation of meaning is a targeted stepped approach to a good life, whatever that means to you.

What is your life's critical pathway?

This diagram shows the journey from the start of a dream to it becoming a reality

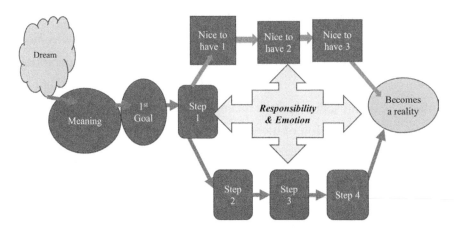

Design your critical path to a dream becoming reality.

Starting at the beginning, you have a dream, you then give it meaning with an end goal to achieve. If you look at the lower arrows, they set the direction of your dream to becoming a reality. The steps 1, 2, 3 and 4 in this example along the lower route are the 'must do' steps. These critical steps are the 'must do' actions that you have to take, to ensure a goal is achieved. They are unavoidable points along your direct of travel towards a goal you have to carry out and address. This is your critical path to a dream becoming reality. Steps 1, 2, 3 and 4 are the objectives you need to achieve along the way before your goal becomes a reality.

This is where the Wheel of a Balanced Life comes in again. Each of your dreams lives within an element of the Wheel of a Balanced Life. My dream house, my dream car, my dream holiday, my dream relationship... Reflect upon **Step 1: Take Responsibility** and Maslow's hierarchy of needs. If your dream is to become healthy and fit, create the critical steps to do that. For example, lose one stone in weight in two months. The critical path is: Step 1 find an exercise you want to do. Step 2 find the equipment or location to do the exercise. Step 3 plan a schedule of exercise and diet. Step 4 design a menu to complement your fitness regime. These steps are the unavoidable critical must-dos. The nice-to-haves are varied and flexible. Nice-to-have 1 could be the type of exercise. Nice-to-have 2 could be what type of equipment you use and the quality of it. Nice-to-have 3 might be the decision about how many days to exercise a week. Nice-to-have 4 could be what type, quality and amount of food you eat and when on your diet over the two months. Then from within the meaning you have created for yourself, take responsibility for it and keep to it, controlling your emotions as your progress to remain positive and upbeat.

So, the upper arrows are the nice-to-haves: the type of house you live in, the type of job you have. Remember, if you live in a house you cannot afford, it is you that have put yourself in that situation. There is an imbalance in your current needs regarding your financial capacity and the house you have dreamed about which has given false meaning to your critical goals. Deal with it; do something about it. Your meaning and the steps towards your goal are yours alone. Having a materialistic mentality is one of the most dangerous aspects of life, as you are presenting yourself to others through what you own rather than who you are. Possessions are temporary; life values are permanent. I am not saying it is wrong to have that car or that house or that life but take responsibility for the goals you set yourself and be careful that they are authentically yours and not emotionally influenced by others. 'Keeping up with the Joneses' is one of the most dangerous emotional influences that can lead you to not live a good life. Get a life; more importantly get *your* life. Disjointed steps along your life's critical path will cause you to drift away from a good life.

From dreams comes meaning. From meaning comes goals. But make sure those goals are clear, honest, authentic and in line with the life you really want. If they are, their effectiveness and quality are reflected in the level of responsibility and commitment you give to the dream, and how you control your emotion along that journey. These are the basics for any good project manager. If you cannot run a project on time and on budget, then your level of success is diluted as a project manager. If you allow the project you manage to drift far from its agreed critical path, it may never become a reality. So become your own project manager in life. The more focussed and the simpler the meaning of your dream, the more powerful it can become. Give power to your life; do not force it. The profoundness of simplicity is the genius in life. And John Lennon was a bit of a genius really. That is why his goals resonate with a lot of people: they did with me.

The creation of meaning is a targeted stepped approach to a living a smarter life and a good life, whatever that means to you. Here are a few tools to help you do that effectively. (Remember this is only a starter for you, so research and read around these suggestions. You could start by exploring the *Bibliography and Notes* at the end of the book.)

Visualisation

Visualisation is something we do subconsciously all the time: what type of meal we want, the holiday we want, the partner we want, the house, the car, the job, the clothes we want to wear, the business we want to build, and how rich we would be if we won the lottery. We put a lot of thought into the life we want.

One of the great visualisations, and probably the most important one that we shy away from and even ignore until it is too late, is the visualisation about our death. At 61, I have the wisdom to know that time is precious and once it is gone it is gone; you cannot get it back.

In my younger years these thoughts did not have so much importance, but they do now and need to be considered, not in a dark way, but positively. At age 20, serving in the Falklands War, and not only seeing my friends lose their lives but also nearly losing mine on a few occasions, gave me an insight into how life can be quickly taken away. Everyone reading this who has been diagnosed with a terminal illness or, like me, has lost someone through cancer, will know what I am on about.

The previous rules of taking responsibility and controlling your emotion come into play here, so do not be scared of that visualisation regarding your death. Many cannot deal with it or blank it from their minds. But really it is the most important of all visualisations, as it forces you to create positive meaning in your life now, while you can still enjoy it. This way, you give yourself a great chance of living the life you want and therefore of dying without regrets. How many people die thinking 'I wish I had done this' or 'why didn't I do that'? Embrace the end-of-life visualisation and think now about how you want to be remembered, and what legacy you want to leave behind. I will talk about this in more detail later in the book.

I have a friend who is a fiduciary financial adviser, Paul Clarke. What he does is help clients come to terms with the philosophy of the life they want, before they even talk about the finances or estate they may have. Then he helps clients create a plan to achieve their good life by figuring out the finances they will need. Such financial advisers are fundamentally different from brokers who have little interest in your life and only want to sell you a policy that a company wants you to buy. A fiduciary financial adviser will tailor the available opportunities around you to give you the best chance in life financially. One of the biggest roles of a fiduciary financial adviser is through the visualisation of retirement. So many people do not want to talk about this, or even think about it; but if you do not visualise your later life needs and the finances required around them, you end up with an inadequate pension to sustain you in the life you want in your later years. Or families are left fighting over the money and assets left when you have gone. Families are torn apart by such lack of visualisation, and governments can take your money and property away from your family if you have not planned adequately. So, visualisation has a powerful role to play in you leaving this earth the way you want to. More importantly, if you believe in an afterlife, you can gaze upon the gifts you have left to the people you love with a smile and a warm feeling of contentment. I'll bet that is a good feeling.

So, visualisation is how you begin to bring your dreams into reality and has been used since the start of time. It is the mental exercise that allows you to form your goals and gives you the best chance to bring them alive sooner rather than later, whether they are big or small. The concept of visualisation attracts some scepticism, but we can use mind power to become successful in every field in our lives. Mental techniques teach us how to use imagination to visualise specific things we wish to have in our lives.

It is quite remarkable how our minds influence our reality. We only use a small percentage of our minds' abilities. We need to learn how to use our natural abilities more effectively. When we visualise where we want to be, those thoughts give us agency. If we recall the process of agency discussed earlier, you 'receive agency' from the image you create in your visualisation. This can then be translated into the creation of meaning. Once meaning is created, you can 'feel the agency' around it. From these thoughts and battles within your mind, you conclude the process by 'taking agency'. If you do nothing with the visualisation, nothing will happen, and you will not take agency from the meaning you have created. However, the opposite is also true. If you do take agency and responsibility for the visualisation you have created, the meaning and direction in your life have a great chance of becoming a reality. Later, I will talk about the power of compounding your decisions, my **Rule 5**, which is the key to ensuring your visualisation becomes a reality.

Visualisation, for our purposes, is the creation of an image that relates to the life you want. If we think of pictures, sounds, emotions, our body will always react in some way to the image. Visualisation, and the image it creates, is the biological and neurological connection between the senses (receiving of agency) and the mind (feeling of agency), through controlling emotions (**Rule 2**): there must be a connection between what you think and the reality around you. That is why meaning must have a personal connection to your mind and body. If you learn to use imagery and visualisation in the right way, it can be an extremely powerful technique to create meaning in your life and allow you to live life smarter.

My YouTube session within the Live Life Smarter Coaching Programme session about how to carry out a visualisation (see *Appendix*) will help you develop this technique, but here is a quick overview:

1. *Frequency*: make sure you continually visualise the image you have in your mind. Keep thinking about that house, that job, the family, that success…

2. *Duration:* keep visualising the image you are trying to create over and over again for at least one, two or three minutes, ideally 15 minutes each time. For me, the most powerful time to do visualisations is early in the morning when my mind is free of life's clutter, or while walking with my dog Dora on the gorgeous Formby beach and through the pine woods.

3. *Vividness*: by doing Step 2, the image will form itself into a tangible and touchable thing. This is where controlling your

emotion is key regarding the meaning you are trying to create in your life from your visualisation. Make sure the image and the meaning you are creating reside in your soul. Do they relate authentically to what you want to do with your life? Will they help you live life smarter and have a chance of being fulfilled?

4. *Intensity:* By following the steps above, the intensity will increase and form meaning, and the image will grow to a point that you can see clear steps and the critical path to the agency you know you need to take. That will bring the image in your mind into reality.

Visualisation can be applied to everything, no matter the size or scale of your thought. Whether you are visualising world peace, eradicating poverty or buying your first home, the creation of meaning through visualisation can be applied to your personal and work life, your health and state of mind, the family and friends you want to have and be with. You can use the creation of meaning for yourself on a personal level, or as a manager, leader, business owner or as a member of a team.

So, start thinking about what you want now, even if you are very young; in fact, doing this when you are young has a more profound effect on your life. The earlier you get your head around this, the more powerful it will be for you. I do understand the difficulty of grasping this when you are young. The key here is the more you practise the creation of meaning, the better and more powerful the habit becomes. So, think about all the things in your life that you want now. Or do you want them in the next few years? What does 'being successful and happy' in life mean to you and what does it look like?

So now we have meaning in life, how do we grow that meaning into becoming a reality? Furthermore, how do we 'take agency' from the 'feeling of agency' process we have created in our minds?

The GROW model

Once you have that dream and you have given it meaning, the key now is to GROW the meaning into your life and make it happen.

The GROW model is a simple method for goal-setting and problem-solving. A good way of thinking about the GROW model is to think about how you would plan a journey. First, you decide where you are going (the goal) and establish where you currently are (the reality). You then explore various routes (the options) to your destination. In the final step, you establish the will to reach your destination. You ensure that you are committed to making the journey and are prepared for the obstacles that you could meet on the way (setting steps for it to happen).

In this process you:

G – Set your **g**oals and identify the problems around them. Take responsibility for a goal, control you emotion around that goal and make sure it has meaning within your life.

R – Recognise your **r**eality relative to your goals and reflect on the importance of your goal to your dreams and desires in life.

O – Consider your **o**ptions. This is the 'feeling of agency' moment. Reflect upon the solutions to each option, choose the best solution and remove the options that will place barriers to you achieving your goals. To help you do this, below is a tool called Mindstorming. This will allow you in a safe way to reflect critically upon and generate the effectiveness and importance of each option.

W– Identify the **way** forward. The 'taking of agency' moment. Select the actions required then time-bind them within your critical pathway to making the meaning of the goal come alive.

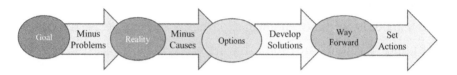

The GROW model

To back up the GROW model now consider using Mindstorming at each step.

Mindstorming

This is a powerful method you can use to unlock your brainpower and generate more ideas for goal attainment. Some people call it 'brain-storming' or 'thought showers'. On a personal level, using this method will make your decisions in life smarter and ultimately more likely to become reality. On a group, team or organisational level, it will make you successful by enabling you to tap into the brainpower of other people. If you do this with an authentic and honest mind, the intensity and vividness of the meaning you are creating in your life will grow upon a solid foundation. These methods are responsible for the creation of many self-made millionaires and blue-chip companies within the Fortune 500 group. You can use the method almost any time and anywhere. So here goes!

The process of Mindstorming is often called the '20 idea method'. It is so powerful in generating ideas that when you begin using it your entire life will change. Those who use it can see immediate profound improvements in every part of their lives to which it is applied. This method is simple, which is probably why it is so powerful. All you need is a blank sheet of paper. At the top of the page, write your current problem or goal in the form of a question. Let us say that your goal is to buy a house within the next nine months. Make the question on this goal as specific as possible. The more specific the question, the better your mind can focus on it, and the better quality of answers you will generate with this exercise.

Mindstorming exercise

Step 1: Write down a focussed question and time-bind it. E.g.: what can I do to move house in the next nine months? Where do I need to live when I finish my degree? How and to whom do I leave my estate/wealth when I die? The simpler the question, the more powerful the exercise is.

Step 2: Let your mind hit the paper. Don't think too much, just empty your head on the paper. Once you think of one thing, it will lead on to another thought. I do this best first thing in the morning or while going for a walk. Sometimes a eureka moment will happen. I never miss those times as they can be profound for what I want to do and achieve in life. Let your mind wander: don't put restrictions on it. Force yourself to give twenty answers to the question at first. The more you do Mindstorming, like everything else in life, the better you become at it. Get the habit now.

Step 3: Now select **any** one of the answers, take action and implement it. Time-bind your action. Create your own critical pathway to make sure the meaning you have created becomes a reality from the goals you have set yourself. When completed, do another one and so on.

Personal contract

A final tool to help you create meaning in your life is to develop your own personal contract. Again, I suggest you look up my YouTube channel Live Life Smarter Coaching Programme (see *Appendix*) and the supporting clip on making a personal contract. Here, I give you a flavour of what it is and what mine means to me, so you can go away and create your own.

Personal Contract for: Dave Armstrong	
Set Date: 4 June 2023	

My Key Personal agreement	To be considered thoughtful and motivated, but true to my word.
My Key functional Skill	I will improve my emotional control and reduce my impulsiveness.
My key role model character	I will show leadership and courage to be who I want to be
My key pathway to growth	Always learning and listening. Never stop.
My Short-term Goal 1	Lose weight to 12.5 stone by December 2023
My Short-term Goal 2	Have my book to the editor by end of October 2023
My Short-term Goal 3	Complete and consolidate this Live Life smarter programme by August 2023
My Long-term Goal 1	To help as many people as I can, to have a life they want before I die
My Long-term Goal 2	To become a recognised author
My Long-term Goal 3	To end my days happy and content with what I have done
My Key Motivational message	
Remove anger and believe everything is possible.	

My personal contract

A key part of creating meaning is the setting of goals from the visualisations you do. The power of a personal contract is that it helps you keep your life on track with meaning. Your personal contract runs across your whole life and will grow as your skill, knowledge and experience in life grow. This chimes with my next **Rule to a Good Life, Rule 4: Keep Learning**. If you want to achieve your personal goals and be the best you can be each day, creating a personal contract will keep you focussed on the pathway towards those goals. A personal contract is a personal commitment to yourself. It is a written one-page statement of what you want to achieve as well as how to achieve it. A personal contract is a powerful self-motivator. It motivates you to create effective habits and set personal values to keep to each day that are in line with your life goals. Whether that is losing weight or running your own business, the general principles of a personal contract cut across every level of your life. Like everything with living a smarter life, the simpler and more achievable the personal contract is, the easier it is to honour. The foundation of the personal contract is set around the character you would like to be and the values you want to live by. The power of the personal contract is in embedding it within your soul and taking responsibility for it in its entirety. The contract you design is solely down to you to fulfil. Do not let yourself down and wonderful things will happen.

So, dream your dreams, visualise them and from them create meaning within all parts of your life. If you let your left brain meet your right brain and use the tools to GROW your life, everything is possible. Take responsibility for all you do, control the emotions around all that, and you will be on the right path to a good life. By creating meaning and setting life goals, you give your life direction. Make sure it is the right direction and that you avoid drift in life. Grab your life now and take responsibility: you will never regret doing so and your future will be yours forever.

Rule 3: Good Life Challenge

a. From this point forward create meaning across all your day-to-day activities and thoughts.

b. Visualise what you want to be and make it happen.

c. Keep the narrative in your mind positive.

d. Keep evolving the meaning you create to continue your growth and success.

Let these statements flow over you and be aware of your drift danger signs. Emotions and feelings you may have:
Procrastination, laziness, idleness, lack of focus, apathy, lethargy, arrogance, distraction, complacency, greed, anger, manipulation, spite, jealousy, and hatred...

And now face the challenge

From now on give every day a purpose by creating meaning for it. Be happy with the day ahead and know what is to be done. It doesn't matter how big or small the targets are during your day, give it your best shot. Make sure the goals you set each day give you a good chance of completing what you intended and that you can deem it successful. Make sure you support your feelings and emotions by creating and maintaining a positive trajectory. Repeating good habits and behaviours over many days ensures you are compounding effective decisions each day. Visualise each day, from the moment you open your eyes to the time you go to sleep. Recognise that with clear meaning within each day the benefits are enormous. Design your own critical path and make sure you complete it. GROW each day and, when stuck, Mindstorm the problems. Set yourself a personal contract, live it and let it flow across all parts of your life. If you are at a low point, you must change the trajectory of your life or you will continue to drift: that is a brutal truth. So, seek to create a different meaning in your life from the current destructive and dark one. Every day give yourself a meaning and purpose that helps you become the better and happier you. Always remember, you are not alone and there is help out there. So go and seek it. Trust me, many people who have created meaning from a low position in life have found enormous success. You can do that too, no matter how low you feel. So, start to become happy with the day ahead and know what is to be done. Recognise and accept that all you do requires thought and planning. Drive yourself to success with clear meaning and clear goals to aim for. Touch, see, taste, hear and smell your goals. Be happy and confident, knowing it is you who drives your self-development towards your goals.

Know that the drive towards your goals is through practice, and more practice, through learning and more learning, through experiences and more experiences. From this, the meaning you have created will give clarity to your future. With clear meaning across each day, anything is possible, and it will lead you to a good life.

RULE 4
TO A GOOD LIFE:

KEEP LEARNING

Why You Need to Keep Learning

The only constant in life is change, so never stop learning.

If you do not keep learning throughout your life, you cannot grow as a person and you will not achieve the life you could have. Change in your life is the primary guaranteed constant. I can hear readers shouting at the book, 'but if it's not broken, don't fix it!' To me, that is such a dangerous statement. In business, high-risk industries and in life, if you really believe that then you leave yourself vulnerable, and through such a mentality you have closed your gateway to learning. Wilfred Emmanuel-Jones (known to many as the Black Farmer) suggests jeopardy and risk are around every corner, and if you do not embrace them and work with them rather than against them, you will have a negative learning trajectory in all aspects of your life.

Let me cut to the chase: you do not learn from the things you do well. You learn from the things you honestly recognise that you do not do well, the mistakes you make. You should constantly look around you for any incremental improvements you can make in the things you do already. Sometimes those observations come from others. Having been fortunate to lecture, train and coach many thousands of people over 30 years in the fire and rescue service, universities and colleges, I say to all the people I come in contact with: if you think you're learning a lot on the course I run, can you image the cumulative effect of all of you on *my* learning? Across every moment of every day, learning opportunities are there, ready and available; you simply need to accept them. Whether it is consolidation of a skill or piece of knowledge, or entering a new experience, grab those moments with both hands.

Let me bring back my friend Albert Einstein who may or may not have said, 'Doing the same thing over and over again and expecting different results each time is insanity'. People think that, by doing the same thing every day, things will change: they will not. Never forget other people will not rest on their laurels and will overtake you, leaving you behind. That goes for friendship, marriages, relationships. If you take your eye off the ball and get complacent in a relationship, one or both partners will drift away. Take responsibility for your life and grab it before the life around you grabs you

Socrates' wise words

Let me return to the great Greek philosopher Socrates who reputedly said these wise words: 'you know the things you know; you know the things you do not know, and you accept and are open to the things you do not know you do not know.'

You know the things you know

That is what every elite performer, athlete or highly successful business person will tell you. Practise, and practise again, the things you know. Arnold Schwarzenegger, actor, film producer, businessman, and politician who served as the 38th governor of California between 2003 and 2011, first became Mr Universe in 1966 and then again in1969. During that time, it was the repetition of exercise every day for many years that got him his titles. I can name many more people who became who they became because they 'knew the things they knew' and formed outstanding habits from that. However, do not think for one minute that they were complacent in their habits. They always avoided been drawn into the attitude of 'if it isn't broken, don't fix it.' They all knew if they stopped looking around and constantly striving to learn at every opportunity from every available source, this would have stopped them achieving what they did. They knew the things they knew and formed outstanding habits around that, tweaking what they did and always striving to get better at it. That is what peak performance is all about: never stop working, never stop growing, never stop learning, and take responsibility for everything you do in life. From this solid mental attitude, you will live life smarter and achieve the good life you want. How does this apply to you? Be honest with yourself. Develop and live good habits.

You know the things you do not know

This is the most powerful quote of the three and is basically saying: keep looking around, keep scanning the life around you and allow your mind to let you know there is something here you sense you do not know about. Having an experience is the 'receiving of agency' moment where what happens around you lands inside your body. You have a feeling that this is new, and you question the current skills, knowledge or experiences you have. I call this the **'gateway to learning'** feeling. Do not be fearful of it, as these are the moments that lead you to live life smarter.

I hate the word 'failure' and have banished it from my life. It has a negative atmosphere around it and creates a destructive trajectory within your mind which can, if you do not control your emotions, lead you to drift, making you doubt yourself. When you feel there is something you do not know or you make a mistake or have an accident, look deep inside yourself, and accept that what has happened has happened and that you at that moment are lacking in some skill, knowledge or experience to deal with it. Be authentic at that moment and try to identify how you can learn from it and move forward. If you drill down into the international standards ISO and Six Sigma, that is all they are: being aware and alive to the things you know you do not know, then finding a direction of travel with actions to deal with your lack of knowledge. So, whether it is as an individual, team or organisation, take responsibility for that moment, as it is yours: control your emotion around it and calm down. Lose your negative thoughts of fear, doubt or embarrassment. Then visualise where you need to be, moderate what you do through the creation of new meaning and set goals to move forward in life and walk through your **gateway of learning**: with a smile.

Sometimes negative feelings will overwhelm you, but stand strong, think critically and accept what has happened is a gift to you for a better future. Trust me: once you grasp these gifts, you will, as Wilfred Emmanuel-Jones suggests, embrace jeopardy and risk in all parts of your life as the fuel to keep you focussed. Accept they play a part in everything you do and give yourself hope by creating meaning for a better and smarter life. If Viktor Frankl can do it as a World War II prisoner of war, you have no excuse.

Please accept you cannot be good at everything; you cannot know everything, and you cannot be expected to do everything. The day you think you can, you bring danger into your future through arrogance and complacency.

You accept the things you do not know you do not know

Socrates suggested when you are at this place you may have wisdom in your life and an enlightened mentality. I am writing this book on my Apple MacBook laptop. If I had lived in the time before Jesus Christ was born and had suggested we could write on a special parchment and, as we wrote, the writing would be presented on other pieces of parchment instantly all across the world, I would have been called a sorcerer. No one would have had the mental capacity to think that one day we might be able to do this; they could not have even imagined it. If you look back in time, many of our great philosophers and scientific geniuses were doubted, disbelieved and many were ostracised by their societies. Socrates himself was condemned to death for daring to challenge his society's status quo.

I know it is hard to step outside the normal but, if you believe what you are doing has an honest, authentic and critical reasoning behind it, then go for it. If you do something only because someone else does, or do it because someone told you to without reason, you live in a dangerous world of unsubstantiated unknown and therefore you are taking up a bystander mentality. That is why gossip and hearsay are a waste of your mental energy. They cause a 'virus' in your mind that will take control if you let it: that is where depression can come from.

I recall the three sieves (filters) of Socrates to help you think straight: truth, good and necessity. Keep learning and keep growing from those around you. Make sure you tap into all the resources available to you. I created my **Rule 6: Work Together** because the cumulative effect of a team or group working together is more powerful than that of an individual working alone. My trusted friends will tell me when I am wrong, but they will not only say it, they will give me evidence that I am wrong. I may not see it at the time, and sometimes the truth is hard to take. But what my friends are doing is forcing me to open my 'gateway to learning', even when I do not see or feel the need to. The people who do this are true friends. When we get on to **Rule 6 – Work Together**, I will talk about my love of having strong characters in my team who will tell me as it is, with evidence. I appreciated and respected having strong union and health and safety representatives within my team and, when I forged bonds of mutual respect, they acted as my 'point people' in a team. I would have been foolish not to consider their alternative viewpoints, as I accept there are some things, I don't know I don't know.

The dangers of not learning as an organisation

I remember when I was getting bullied by senior managers in the fire service in 2005 for daring to challenge the status quo of modernisation of the fire service. My role in a small strategic advisory team working directly to the Chief Fire Officer was research and development of structures to help the modernisation project set a pathway for a realignment of the fire service to move from a rank-based organisation to a role-based organisation. The evidence-based findings from that project, although reliable and valid, were out of line with what senior managers wanted to hear as the findings were rather raw in their conclusion and did not show senior culture in a good light. Conflicting leadership styles, authoritarian management style, lack of diversity understanding, and silo-working, to name but four, were evident across the brigade. Silo working is when people are not working together; and avoid sharing, knowledge, skills and experience, for the greater good.

They believed I was not following the project directives and presenting the brigade in a bad light. The previous Audit Commission inspection had already issued a poor performance mark on the brigade, one of the issues then being that the brigade's own report focussed only on what they were good at and could do, rather than what were the known risks and issues. All the senior team wanted me to do was blindly follow them without argument and show them in a good light: all without reason or justification and with little or no supporting evidence from them. However, the project ended with the brigade receiving a revised Audit Commission mark of good to outstanding performance, following our work.

That's when the bullying started, as the senior officers regrouped post-project and began to ostracised me from the brigade management team. I requested and was allowed a meeting with three of my bullies a year and a half after the project concluded, after being manipulated down from a high-rank officer to much lower one. My house had been repossessed and I had been forced to enter a financial voluntary arrangement (IVA). I was told at the meeting I did not fit in and that I was disloyal and this was why I was not being given opportunities to advance my career anymore.

I replied to the accusation like this: 'I find that confusing as I believe I am more loyal than you know. If the three of you were walking across the road, chatting and oblivious that a car was about to crash into you, I would run and push you all out of the way into a thorn bush to save your lives. The car would disappear into the sunset and all you would be able to see and feel would be me pushing you into a bush and hurting you without clear reason, unaware I had saved your lives. Most people who you promote will not challenge you, will not argue with you, for fear of reducing their chances of promotion or career advancement. That to me is disloyalty and they would let you get run over. I will save your life even though it hurts you, and ultimately me. Now *that* is loyalty.' In short, I would be saving them from **the things they did not know they did not know.**

The point I am making here is that, in order for them to be sustainable and successful, corporations and businesses must keep learning and have an open and trusting culture across all levels that joined-up learning is part of day-to-day life. That is, everyone in the organisation is working together towards common goals. I have found that people and groups who shy away from audits do not really understand their importance. Corporate audits assess strategic (top), tactical (middle) and task (lower) presentations of an organisation's systems, processes and communication. Basically, the strategic position an organisation presents to an audit should demonstrate it is fully aware of what is happening on the shop floor in regard to what they produce or how they perform. If there is a gap between what people do on the shop floor and what the strategic documents paint to the auditors, the organisation will be marked as poorly performing. However, if the strategic story reflects the real shop floor story, and they can demonstrate a clear direction of travel to address known risk and lack of learning, the organisation will be marked with excellent performance as it has demonstrated it clearly knows its risks, it is managing them to prevent them becoming issues and it has clear plans to resolve them contained in a one-, three or five-year plan.

I know this is a dark story, but I was not angry with the way I was treated, only heartbroken. It is sad that some people in influential positions focus more on money, power and their own pensions than they do on doing the right thing. They are ignorant of or blinkered to the damage they can do to lots of people beneath them and the organisation's reputation strategically. Sadly, I have to some degree been proved right as many private and public sector organisations since

2005 have chosen profit through savings and cutbacks rather than to deal with known risks in the first instance, allowing them to grow and become issues at a corporate level. The big shift in culture in the UK in 2005 was that the government changed their emphasis from direct enforcement and inspection to self-assessment of risks for all organisations. The problem with this is, when money is tight training is the first budget generally to go. And once you start the avoidance of risk and dilute continual learning, the problems from that will compound over time. Sadly, this avoidance of known risks is only really addressed when something goes wrong; on many occasions with tragic and disastrous consequences. We only have to look at the problems in the UK National Health Service today to see this. We will talk more about this later when we come to my **Rule 5: Compounding Decisions**

On an individual level, the same process will apply. In your private life you may have people who tell you what you are doing is not healthy, that there is risk or there is an issue to be addressed. But they tell you out of loyalty and offer you substantiated evidence to support their view. So, develop the things you know you know for yourself. Put your hands up when there are things around you that you know you do not know. And accept that there are some things in your current life you do not know you do not know and therefore cannot see, feel or think about them.

The simple solution to this conundrum is to keep learning across every experience and at every opportunity. Develop excellent habits, **keep that learning gate open** and be wise in what you do and think. Do not be frightened: see these unknown unknowns as gifts and opportunities to live life smarter. As Charles Darwin[41] taught us, it is not the strongest of the species that survives, nor the most intelligent, but the one most adaptable to change. Keep learning.

How Do You Keep Learning?

Marcus Aurelius was Roman Emperor from 161 to 180 and was seen as a Stoic philosopher. In fact, he is known as the philosopher king. The reason he was so successful, it could be suggested, was because he never stopped learning and never got arrogant with his power, even to the extent that he would keep someone near him to remind him when required that he was a mere mortal not a god. He wrote twelve books that he called *Meditations*. He used these books as a reference for his own guidance and continual learning. He never relied only on his memory and referred to previous notes to make decisions in both the society he lived and the battles he fought. He was a critical thinker in everything he did and grew his knowledge and skill set across all he did. I want to break this down and give you an insight into what it means, so you too can keep learning.

Intellectual capital

I urge you to develop your **intellectual capital** which complements spiritual intelligence which I covered earlier. When you are born, you feed your brain through your senses from the minute you open your eyes. In your formative years you are vulnerable to your parents and the people around you. But once your brain begins to process and you start to join the dots, so to speak, you begin to reason and make judgements. From that point, your left brain and right brain will develop, and your habits and behaviours are beginning to form. There are three areas you need to be aware of to build your intellectual capital.

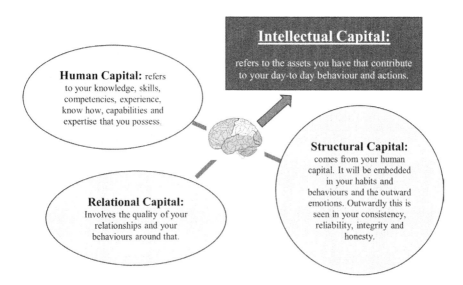

Intellectual Capital

Human capital

This refers to the development of your knowledge, skills, competencies, experiences, capabilities and what expertise you have. This can take any form, as the beauty of life is that we are all different, and our experiences vary. My friend Basil Reynolds[42] talks about this in his book *Finding Your Music Inside*. Recognise what you love doing, what excites you, what gets you out of bed in the morning and what you feel you are most at home with. Once you find your music inside, build your human capital around it. Take responsibility for it, control your emotions and create meaning to achieve it. And never stop learning on the way so you continually improve throughout your life. Remember: if you do something only once, you will forget what you did virtually instantly. However, if you repeat that action over and over again, you will form an embedded habit. This is what peak performers do, and once the habit is formed, the action they carry out is done without thinking. It enters their senses as a natural habit and behaviour and, as we discussed earlier, they become spiritually intelligent.

Relational capital

This involves the quality you give and settle for in your relationships and, from that, what behaviours you develop in your relationships. I know at times I have let toxic people into my life who have little interest in me. Those people have different music inside them and are not a good match for me. They have different values from mine. It was not until I was 45 that I realised my life is solely my responsibility and how I live it is down to me. I recognised that if I do not understand myself and become proud of myself, like myself and even love myself, then how can I really offer any of that to others? I do not think I am better than anyone else; I have simply found a space to be me without arrogance. I can hold my head up and say my values have stayed with me to this day, and so I can write this book. Sometimes sticking to my values has had a destructive short-term effect on me, as I described earlier, but the longevity of solid values in life will serve you well.

So, developing your relational capital is how you choose the people in your life and the quality of the relationships you form, be they partnerships, friendships, work or team relationships. If you respect difference and celebrate the beauty of diversity, then you will not go far wrong.

Structural capital

This brings it all together and is formed in your habits and behaviours. When you have high structural capital, this is seen in the values you live by and in the consistency and reliability you demonstrate through the honesty and integrity evident to the outside world. By building your human and relational capital, you grow the structural capital that ultimately adds to your level of overall intellectual capital. You will see and feel the relationship of this to your intellectual intelligence (IQ) and your emotional intelligence (EQ) and how it ultimately grows your spiritual intelligence (SQ). Keep learning in every area to harmonise both sides of the brain and improve your intellectual capital and spiritual intelligence. By working on both the logical and creative sides of your brain you will live life smarter and find a good life.

Let us look at what peak performers actually do in regard to keeping learning, as we can learn so much from them. Peak performers give everything their complete concentration to consistently perform to the maximum of their ability: intellectually, mentally and physically. Peak performance is characterised by feelings of confidence and effortlessness: what some people call the 'flow zone' or 'sixth sense'. Therefore, harmonising your emotions, feelings and attitude is key to achieving peak performance. Peak performance is making sure you leave no stone unturned by taking responsibility for everything you do. Elite sports and business people make sure every element of their performance is analysed and has meaning so they can perform consistently to the best of their ability and have an idea of where they are heading. They focus on every element of their performance, incrementally growing each of those elements to become the best they can be. The key then is to recognise that you can continually learn and grow, adding value to what you do today for tomorrow. Having the right attitude enables you to focus and maintain your momentum so you can get the results you are aiming for. You can apply these ideals to any part of your life and to any level of life, but it is down to you.

Ultimately, if you keep learning, you may embed the wisdom of Socrates whereby you accept and are open to the things you do not know you do not know. You will be truly wise when you are happy with and accept that your past is all you have experienced before. Remember, you cannot change the past, but you can learn from it to make a better future. Be happy in what you do today. Recognise and accept that all you do today is done to the best of your current ability, knowledge and experience. There is no such thing as failure: it is just a moment in time when you need to open your gateway to learning. Finally recognise and embrace that there is always room for improvement. So, keep learning: it is a lovely feeling.

Remember, if you have high spiritual and intellectual levels, you can become truly wise. But, as Socrates intimated, a wise person will never admit they are wise. That is for others to observe and comment on. It is your habits, behaviours and attitudes that dictate whether you become wise and enlightened. This is the ultimate level of life to strive for to live a good life. Be open and honest with yourself and keep on learning. You will get there if you really want to.

In summary: keep learning; never stop! Make sure you get something out of every day. Remove failure from your mind and, when things do not go well, see them as learning gifts. Keep that learning gate open at all times. Grab your life now and take responsibility for it. You will never regret doing so and your future will be yours forever.

Rule 4: Good Life Challenge

a. Keep on learning and build your intellectual capital.

b. Always have your 'gateway to learning' open – never close it!

c. Keep learning across all your day-to-day activities and thoughts.

d. If in doubt, learn something new.

e. Reboot your learning habits continually.

f. Never stop growing your happiness and success.

Let these statements flow over you and be aware of your drift danger signs. You may experience any of these emotions:

Procrastination, boredom, little interest in your surroundings, arrogance, ignorance, avoidance, fear of experience, fear of learning, anger, manipulation, distraction, complacency and ego.

And now face the challenge

Wake up each day and try to learn something new or at least develop something in your life for the better. Know that learning is the key ingredient to your future success and it drives you towards living the good life. Each day, build your intellectual capital by growing your human capital. Look to every opportunity to develop your knowledge, skills, competencies, experiences, capabilities and expertise. Build your relational capital by getting to know and learning from the people around you, by enjoying or improving your relationships. Most importantly, respect difference, celebrate the beauty of diversity and learn from alternative views and thoughts.

If you are feeling low or leading a destructive life, know that learning to do something different now, or to do something better, is the key to addressing how you begin the journey towards a good life. Do not say that you cannot do this: you can. Change the story in your mind. Say: what can I do or learn to do today for my better tomorrow?

Remove failure from your vocabulary and replace it with 'a moment to learn'. Recognise, when things do not go so well, it is a golden opportunity to 'go again' by learning a new skill, developing an old one, gaining more knowledge or seeking a different experience to grow. Never get too carried away with success or too down when things do not go well. Know that, whatever you have worked on and learned in that day, you gave it your best. Recognise learning is as important as eating: it is mental nourishment.

So, keep growing the things 'you know you know', always look to develop the things 'you know that you don't know' and give respect to and be open to the things 'you don't know you don't know'.

Remember, the 'fuel' for a good life is to learn something new each day, embrace it and smile while you are doing it. Always keep your gateway to learning open.

RULE 5
TO A GOOD LIFE:

COMPOUND DECISIONS

Why You Must Compound Good Decisions
The only way to change habits and behaviours is by compounding effective decisions.

You may have heard the saying 'stay ahead of the curve'. Like most things in my life, I was taught this when I joined the Royal Navy Fleet Air Arm in 1979 as a 17-year-old and it has never left me. It was embedded into me to keep learning and keep growing as a person by not allowing myself to drift in life. We all do it in some form or another, whether losing weight, keeping a relationship strong, enjoying the job you are doing, running a business, team or organisation. But it is the compounding of your decisions that is so important to keeping learning and living life smarter.

I have passed on those teachings from 1979 to all the people and teams I have been fortunate to be allowed to help and lead on their growth journeys, both in the fire and rescue service and in education. Stay ahead of the curve by always striving to improve and compound good habits. It is the compounding effect of the decisions you make and then enact that is fundamentally key to your present and future good life in regard to your health, knowledge, happiness, love, career and success.

First, let me talk about repetition. I used to say to my students after the first day's input: 'once you leave this room you will forget my name; once you are on the stairs you will forget what we talked about; and when you leave the building, you won't even think about what you were here for, as your life will take your mind away.' After the initial chuckle from them, I wanted to make them aware of and get them to think about the natural drift in life and how it happens without thinking if you do not control it and if you do not keep practising to hold it at bay. As the old adage suggests: if you don't use it, you will lose it. By making yourself aware of this natural mental habit, you are slowing or even stopping your memory curve from drifting.

Forgetting to remember is a natural human trait so understanding the **sigmoid curve** gives you a simple mental framework that prevents or reduces that drift happening in the first place. In simple behavioural terms, the sigmoid curve is a model that helps you to address times when you have a dip in life or something goes astray. It tells you to stop and catch yourself before you drift too far from a good position. Catch yourself before you allow that drift to grow.

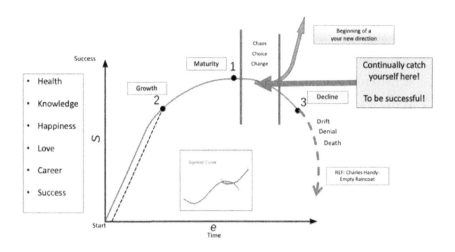

The Sigmoid Curve

The sigmoid curve tells us that if you embrace an experience. good or bad. and deal with it in its first instance authentically and honestly, your skills and knowledge will grow positively from that point so you can continue your journey to self-actualisation and maturity, managing your peaks and troughs. Once you grab this sigmoid curve skill and it becomes set in your subconscious, it then becomes a skill you practise without thinking, a good habit you can repeat.

Think about the first time you drove a car. You thought about the peddles, brakes, gears and mirrors, and you were initially awkward in using them all. But each time you drove, the need to work all these elements moved further to the back of your mind as you increased your skill and became more comfortable with driving; until you reached the point that it became a natural habit that required little thinking.

Through the repetition of good skills and knowledge, you forge in your body and mind good habits and behaviours. Jonny Wilkinson kicked the ball in the final seconds of the final match to win the World Cup. The habits, skills and techniques Jonny showed in that moment, and the split-second decision to employ them, came from the accumulation and compounding of practice over and over again. This compounding allowed him to behave as naturally as if he was on a public field playing with his kids.

Many peak performers, in whatever field of skill, will tell you that this a wonderful place to be. Many call it the 'sweet spot' or being 'in the zone'. Remember, you are building and compounding your intellectual and emotional skills to become spiritually intelligent to drive the things you do. You have also built your intellectual capital around that skill by bringing the left and right brain together. In addition, you are processing the elements of agency within your mind. Your desire, your hunger, to drive the car or kick that goal, are the source of agency. These feelings of agency fluctuate from awkwardness to confidence and, when you start the car or kick that ball, you are taking the agency and making the decision to act (or not to act). The more you open your gateway to learning and give yourself experiences, the better you become.

The elements of the sigmoid curve are eloquently presented by Charles Handy, an Irish author and philosopher who specialised in organisational behaviour and management, in his book *The Empty Raincoat*. His illustration shows that time never stops but your levels of success dip up and down through life dependent on what responsibility you take, the emotion you control and the meaning you give to what you do. So, catch yourself when you begin to drift and always be open to new experience, change and learning. Try, when you feel change around you, to begin a new curve and push yourself towards a positive trajectory.

It is important to understand the power of compounding decsions because the habits you form and how you continually learn from them are key to your personal, team and organisational success.

In business it is not just very important, it is *essential* to compound decisions to stay ahead of the curve, as the principles and understanding of the sigmoid curve are embedded around the world by successful organisations, and used by Fortune 500 companies, governments and political groups.

> **Doing lots of intelligent, positive, different things to get results**
> **= SANITY**
>
> —Dave Armstrong

We all experience periods of drift and gain across our own Wheels of a Balanced Life, but please remember that we keep on that positive trajectory by taking responsibility each day for what we do, by controlling our emotion, by making sure we have meaning in everything we do and that we keep on learning. The compounding of our decisions from that learning gives us the best chance to live life smarter. We must keep catching ourselves on the downward curve before we drift too much.

How Do You Compound Decisions?

Scott Snook serves as a professor in the Department of Behavioural Sciences and Leadership at the United States Military Academy and is a senior lecturer at Harvard Business School. He presented a theory that, if you uncouple from a system design and drift away from the required base line performance, then drift in operational performance will naturally happen.

If we reflect upon the work of Charles Perrow, we can take that one step further. Charles Perrow was a professor of sociology at Yale University and visiting professor at Stanford University. His work suggested that accidents are normal within complex environments, which echoes the theories regarding jeopardy held by William Emmanuel-Jones, the Black Farmer. Charles Perrow stated that multiple and unexpected failures are catastrophes waiting to happen. An accident, crisis or disaster is simply an initial risk ignored or avoided and allowed to compound into an issue.

In 1984, Perrow researched the disaster at Three Mile Island[43]. This accident involved the partial meltdown of the Three Mile Island Unit Two nuclear reactor in Pennsylvania, United States, on March 28, 1979. Today it is still one of the most significant accidents in the United States' commercial nuclear power plant history. In doing this work, Perrow established what he called Normal Accident Theory: a situation where the systems involved were so complex and tightly coupled that an accident was, perhaps, the inevitable outcome.

So, bear with me here as I look at the consequences of this on a large-scale example before I examine how compounding decisions helps you or hinders you at a personal level. Think about the Grenfell Fire in London UK on 14 June 2017. A high-rise fire broke out in the 24-storey Grenfell Tower block of flats in North Kensington. Seventy two people died, with many hundreds injured, not to mention the many scarred for life mentally.

It was the residents left alone who watched the deterioration of Grenfell Tower over many years before anyone else noticed its poor state, then chose to ignore it and do nothing. Sadly, the residents did not have the skill set nor the authority to sort the problems out themselves, and, when they raised their fears, their pleas fell on deaf ears. The organisations who should have been responsible for intervening did not listen to the residents' concerns about a variety of increasing risks and issues. Government had introduced fire safety self-assessment in a 2005 modernisation of public services, forcing the drastic and nearly complete destruction of fire safety enforcement and auditing. I believe a senior local authority leader consulted a fire safety advisor after the Grenfell Fire occurred, saying, 'let's get all the enforcement officers and building control officers out there and start inspecting.' The answer from the advisor was 'there aren't any'. They had all been redistributed to private industry as the requirement was now for self-assessment, not enforcement, so there was no need to fund them. In addition, the local social services did not help the residents as well as they could once have done, due to cutbacks. The owners of the tower block knew they would not be audited as much, so profit margins were pushed and maintenance was either shifted or not completed. I can hear readers shouting at the book, 'but this and that is wrong'. That is not the point I am making here. The reason the Grenfell Fire happened was that the building, for whatever reason, was allowed to drift away from its operational performance and standard. It became so unsafe the fire was inevitable from the compounding of decisions not to intervene in that drift. In essence, no one talked together. The accident (fire) was always going happen one day. As Charles Perrow suggests, it was a normal accident; a predictable incident. As Scott Snook's work suggests, you will always need to be vigilant to stay above the curve, in particular when there are lots of complex environments involved, because if you drift away from the operational standard catastrophe is just around the corner. However, it could have all been avoided by simply changing the trajectory of the behaviours to a positive constructive one with honesty, trust and integrity, and by working as a team rather than a bunch of individuals. There was silo-working across the parties involved with Grenfell. History is littered with these types of events.

A simple accident, to a disaster or catastrophe, all stem from a simple risk that is allowed to compound and be ignored. The signals and signs are all there and once ignored the compounding effect will take place. Bradford City football stadium fire[44] (1985): 56 died. The Kings Cross London Tube disaster[45] (1987): 31 died. Both caused by the build-up of rubbish. At Bradford the rubbish was under the stand; at Kings Cross it was under an escalator. People had raised concerns about the rubbish buildup many years before: the risk was ignored. Even with the Hillsborough football disaster in 1989, when 97 Liverpool fans died, the warnings had been there in 1987 during a match between Leeds and Coventry City. Leeds fans had a near-miss. Even as far back as 1981, in a football match between Tottenham Hotspur and Wolverhampton Wanderers, the warning signs were there. Tottenham fans had been forced to spill onto the pitch from the Leppings Lane end of the ground due to the crushing of people. Both these near-misses happened in the same area as the Hillsborough tragedy unfolded. Scarily, as I write this today there are once again reports of a near-miss during a match between Sheffield Wednesday and Newcastle United with many Newcastle fans being crushed in the Leppings Lane end of the ground. Madness, or should I say 'insanity'?

I was a follower of Punk Rock in the 1970s and a band I liked was the Sex Pistols (although my favourite was The Clash). The Sex Pistols were not everyone's cup of tea. They were raw, rebellious and in your face, seen as anti-establishment. Many years later on 25 September 2015, during an interview with television presenter and journalist Piers Morgan[46], John Lydon (alias Jonny Rotten of the Sex Pistols) was asked about Jimmy Savile[47], the prolific sex abuser, who, before his fall from grace, had been the BBC's top man presenting shows like *Jim'll Fix It* and the iconic *Top of the Pops* which both gave him access to children. *Top of the Pops* was where John and Savile met.

Straight away, the 'anti-establishment' band reported to others Savile's evil deeds and expressed the disgust they had for what they called 'a little pervert'. Their claims fell on deaf ears. Like the Grenfell Tower residents, they were not taken seriously and were ignored. They had dared to challenge the establishment of which Jimmy Savile was a part at that time. So, all the warning signs were ignored and Savile's evil compounding of abuse was allowed to go on unchallenged, apparently because of his status in the BBC and nationally. Consequently, many children and young adults suffered from the ignorance and bystander attitude of others. It is a weird human trait that, when we allow events to negatively compound in our lives, we have to wait for a tragedy to happen before we do something about it. Compounding decisions has momentum; you choose which way it goes. I choose gain over drift.

I was lucky to teach for many years at college and university. I used to ask the question: 'what is the best accident to have?' Virtually every time, the reaction was confusion. Of course, there is no best accident. The actual answer is the best accident to have, is the one in your head. That is the one that has not yet happened but you know could happen. Commonly this is known as a risk. As Socrates said, 'you know the things you know,' and this is the potential incident or accident you are aware of. Importantly, nothing has happened as yet. But, if ignored or avoided, over time the compounding effect of that ignorance and avoidance becomes a near-miss. Then, if still ignored and avoided, it becomes an incident. Then, if it is still ignored and avoided, it ultimately ends up with injury and death.

The point I am making here is you need to raise your fist, become your own 'point person' in life and always respond to the concern in your mind at the first instant; particularly if what you are doing or seeing around you is giving you a feeling of fear, dread, doubt or wrong-doing. When you are putting on weight, getting unfit or feeling worry and discomfort, do not let those thoughts and emotions grow to the extent they become an issue and ultimately end as an incident. Humans have a habit of avoidance or ignorance when it comes to destructive feelings and thoughts, and we allow them to compound over time unchecked. But at some point, they will have to be addressed. You do not have to fall into this habit. When you get those feelings, make them your learning gifts and think about what you should do differently *now*, what you should learn and whether you could open yourself up to a different experience.

If you are alive to and open to learning, all the signs are there, and known risks must not go ignored or avoided. I am not telling you something that has not been said before. Although I am spiritual rather than religious, I still respect and read religious texts as they all have wisdom and warnings within them on how to lead a good life. Even Jesus Christ at his death on the cross says: '*Father, forgive them because they do not know what they do*'[48]. Today's examples of such ignorance are the issues around climate change and the stupidity of anger and war. Please listen to the risks being raised now, take responsibility for the feelings they evoke, control your emotion and, for our children's and grandchildren's sakes, do not ignore the risks. We all owe it to them to protect them by addressing risk in the first instant together, and effectively compound our decisions today and so we can avoid the potential disasters of tomorrow.

So, you may now be saying: what has this got to do with my personal life? Everything! The basics of human behaviour are there for you to tap into; you simply need to first be able to see them, and second have the honesty and authenticity to do something about it. That's it. In every moment of the day the 'receiving of agency' happens all around you. It is for you to see it and bring it into your body through your senses, so you can start the 'feeling of agency' process within your mind.

The good news is: here you are, reading this and there is the good life ahead of you if you want it. Wherever you are in life, whether you are drifting or gaining is for you to decide. If you keep on the negative trajectory, you must 'mind the gap'. Do not kid yourself: accidents and incidents will happen if you do not change your trajectory. If you have no plan, you are drifting in life. Right this minute as you read this, if you choose to take responsibility for all areas of your life, you can change the trajectory and develop gain in life. Be honest, authentic and true to yourself and control the emotions around that. Consider each element within the Wheel of a Balanced Life and create meaning for each one. Open your mind to new things and experiences and begin to learn from them. From that, keep practising and repeating the positive and constructive new things and start compounding your habits and behaviours to give yourself a new life.

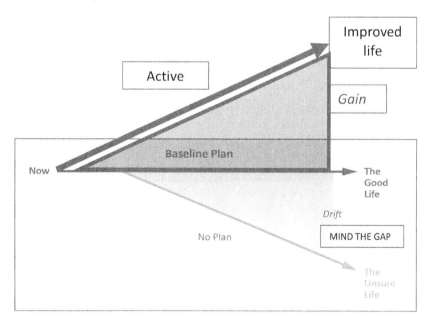

'Mind the Gap': between a good life and an unsure life.

Now here is the tough bit: there are no excuses. Just start compounding the decisions you make on the journey to a better life. It is not an easy journey but, if you stick with it, it will lead you to live life smarter and help you lead a good life.

Decision-making and then taking action (or not)

The definitions and ideology around what is a decision, and what is the decision-making process are confusing. So here goes. **Decision-making** is fundamentally different from the **decision taken**; it is a profound difference. **Decision-making** is everything you do before you **take a decision**. Every **decision we take** is a singular moment in time. The decision-making process ends in a single action or choice taken or not taken. Go back to the cake example. After the feeling of agency, the decision-making process leads to the action of eating the cake or not eating the cake. Both are decisions taken after the brain has led you to take action or no action. Remember, every constructively positive decision taken that you compound together optimises your learning to a better future. If you make a destructive negative decision and compound it, you are heading towards a worse future. It is that simple.

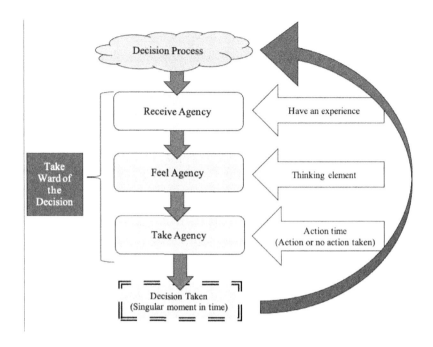

The Decision Process

Decision-making happens anywhere and at any time for any reason through the process of agency. So, decision-making is simply the research and feeling element of decisions. The decision taken is the singular moment that you action and it cannot be changed, as it has happened in a moment in time.

So let me take this one step further. A decision you take and action is the same as a decision you take with no action. It is a choice you take in that instant to do something or do nothing. Taking no action is like bystander mentality: you have taken the decision to do nothing as you let things happen. You are *accepting the situation and maintaining the status quo*.

Think of this: if a fight broke out and your child was involved and you decided to do nothing, the fight would continue. So, by doing nothing, you become a bystander, accepting the status quo and you allow the situation to continue. It is like if you do not vote: you are actually voting for the status quo. This is what politicians play on, people not voting. It is an *active* response to not get involved.

At this point, I strongly suggest you research and watch the excellent BBC documentary *The Five Steps to Tyranny*[49]. It covers the work of academics such as Professor Stanley Milgram[50] and Philip Zimbardo[51], and the poignant conclusion of the documentary is that tyranny is the ultimate product of compounding anger and hatred. However, if you stop it at its first step, the creation of an 'us and them', tyranny cannot grow or even exist. If you create an 'us and them', introducing a difference or prejudice with the intention of influencing a move towards a negative and angry trajectory or position, the compounding domino effect of that is people's positions become different and the gap grows between them within an angry and negative environment. Conflict and wars are the consequences of this.

So, why don't we simply change the narrative of that story in the first instance to work together rather than working apart (my **Rule 6: Work Together**)? I recommend some thinkers who can explain this issue in greater depth: the aforementioned Professors Stanley Milgram and Phillip Zimbardo, and Solomon Asche[52]. These academics have researched the dangers and manipulation of conformality and obedience. Please look up their experiments. One involves a train and giving up a seat, another involves judging the length of a line within a group. There is one where volunteers electrocute strangers. And the most well known is the Stanford Prison experiment where Phillip Zimbardo got volunteers off the street to spend time in a prison environment where they were either placed as guards or prisoners. I would also suggest you look up the blue eyes/brown eyes experiment by Jane Elliot[53], created following the death of Dr Martin Luther King[54], in which she tried to explain his assassination to the class of young children she taught at the time. These experiments show how the mind can be manipulated and controlled to obey or simply conform to orders and be sucked into environments with dark and destructive consequences. You only have to look at the actions and power of Adolf Hitler during the Second World War to see the extent and scale to which such manipulation can be used with the ultimate of destructive force.

On an individual level, the taking of agency is a decision you take with an action or a decision you take with no action. Conformity and obedience lie generally on the side of a negative destructive no-action, but please note that on occasions saying nothing or doing nothing can be a powerful statement of intent and unselfishness as mentioned in the chapter on **Rule 2: Control Your Emotion.**

WARNING

It is your responsibility whether the agency you take is to do nothing or something, even if you have a feeling that the action or non-action you take is not what you really want to do. The responsibility for doing that will always be yours. What you do in the negative context within your mind is called a *wilful lie* to yourself. Remember, ultimately, when you lie or cheat the only person you are doing it to is yourself.

The bottom line for self-responsibility is to be the 'ward', the owner and custodian, of all you do. So always remember and accept that your position of self-responsibility will never change. You will think 'I *have* to do this' because 'my family depend on it', 'my job depends on it', or even 'my life depends on it'. But, if you do make and then take a decision you are not happy with, expect that you will begin to drift in life as you are compounding negative and destructive decisions. Be aware that negative trajectory usually does not stop until something dramatic happens; a disaster occurs that involves people being injured and, on many occasions, dying.

Sadly, I have lost two friends to who took their own lives, which is the worst compounding drift in life. On both occasions, I was saddened and disappointed in myself as I never saw it coming. I wish I could have five minutes with them now. The taking of one's own life comes from a negative mental trajectory where a person reaches such a mental low that they can see only a dead end with no other way out. Trust me, there is always an alternative. This is what my first rule is about: take responsibility for yourself now and begin the journey to a better and good life, no matter how bad you think things are. Even if you take one single thing at first to be responsible for, it's a start.

When I slept on Euston train station in 2007, I did contemplate killing myself, but there is a certain person in my life who stops me each time from going down that route. In fact, he is the person I try to live my life to the full each day for. You could call him my guardian angel. But who that person is and the profound role he has played in my life is for the end of this book.

The final part of compounding decisions is that not remembering a decision taken, not taking responsibility for that decision taken, will lead to blame, doubt and repeating of mistakes. So do not underestimate the power of remembering the decisions you have taken as they consolidate the compounding of a positive trajectory towards your good life. Emperor Marcus Aurelius consolidated most decisions he took in what are known as his *Meditations*. So, when he prepared to a take a new decision, he would look up a previous decision he had taken, reflect upon it and either action it again or moderate that decision to improve it. In the modern day, we might call this continual professional development. This process is embedded in international standards such as IOS and Six Sigma, and UK bodies such as the education standards committee OFSTED[55], and health and safety regimes. They all live in this 'never forget to remember' learning process. Even our UK legal system has a process called the 'setting of precedent' whereby, when new cases are brought forward, decisions taken in the past can be used as benchmarks for future decisions. This is why the UK legal system is the most revered on our planet, as it is based upon the compounding of decisions for a better future.

You may be asking: what has all this got to do with me and my life? It has everything to do with it. The process of compounding decisions is *exactly the same* for you to lead a good life as it is for a company working together and being successful, or a country or planet growing its laws, habits and behaviours. Everything we do in life can be linked back to our five senses and the agency moments we receive through the experiences we expose ourselves to. The cumulative and compounding effect of the actions we take from those experiences is affected by how we control our emotion when we arrive at the 'feeling of agency' process. So please recognise that the overall effect of 'compounding decisions' in regard to actions we take or don't take comes from the behaviours and habits we form from the three-stage agency process.

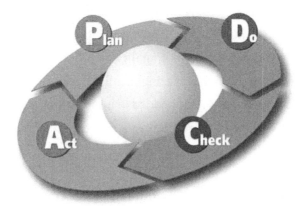

Plan – Do – Check – Act
Deming PDCA (Plan, Do, Check, Act) cycle

Let me now talk about a big point in history where the compounding of a good decision was really looked at. The Deming PDCA (Plan, Do, Check, Act) cycle[56] was developed after the Second World War when the Americans met the Japanese. It was then when quality and standards systems really started to develop, for instance Total Quality Management (TQM) and ideologies such 'Just in Time', commonly known as JIT[57]. It was the first time that people looked at compounding decisions and sharing them within large systems. The Japanese were more focussed on what they could improve upon, how they could become more efficient, rather than saying how good they were. Then came the Andon (pull) cord which is now embedded in many high-performing companies. Basically, it is a bit like being 'point'. If you see a fault, accident, incident, or if you think something could happen or see something that could be done better, you pull the cord.

Most importantly, there are *no* adverse consequences for you in pulling the cord (putting your hand up) as you are being honest and authentic. So, there is no reason *not* to pull the cord as it leads to the company having a continuous improvement culture across all levels of its organisation. Everyone sees and feels that they are part of the team's overall success whatever their role may be. Some companies go further, with the opposite emphasis: if you are found to have hidden or ignored a known risk or potential improvement and did not pull the cord, this can lead to your dismissal. There is no reason to hide risks if you see them, as there is 'no blame' attached to honesty.

You should now appreciate the power of working together (Rule 6) for the future good, betterment and job security of a team. From those humble beginnings in the 1950s, we now see such systems as Six Sigma. Like Just in Time (JIT), it looks at how to become lean in all you do. JIT is a process that examines how you can get the right amount of equipment, resources and people all at the right time, at the production end of a products' build or service supplied. This then cuts costs on stowage of large amounts of unproductive stock and people. Six Sigma looks at waste reduction across all areas: the company's inventory of items, people and talent; waiting times; the movement of people within a system; reducing defects; transportation of items, goods and people; overprocessing or repeating of actions, and over-production of a product or service.

WARNING

Some companies use JIT and Six Sigma in totally the wrong way. They see them as tools to implement their philosophy that minimum amount of equipment, resources and people equals maximum profit. If they take their eyes off the ball regarding sustainability and long-term strategy, they can and will come a cropper.

The disadvantages of JIT or Six Sigma systems involve potentially dangerous disruptions in the supply chain if the focus is away from sustainable quality. If a supplier has a breakdown and cannot deliver the goods promptly, or they have not got enough people to perform and deliver the service, this could stall and collapse the entire production line or business. A sudden unexpected order for goods or demand on service may delay the delivery of finished products to clients and customers. If we look at the problems with public services today, it seems that situation has evolved over many years of cutting the cloth too much under pressure to do more for less; politicians called it *austerity*. If you underfund or undersupply a system incorrectly, it will collapse one day. Again, it is a risk or danger initially ignored or avoided that causes the future problems and issues. Recognise now that to take responsibility for all your decisions taken, is the engine of your learning and also leads you faster to the goals you have set for betterment in the future. The constructive positive compounding of your decisions taken will give you the good life as you strive for a sustainable future, whether that be for yourself or the teams you work within; irrespective of their size or scale.

Decision-taken process

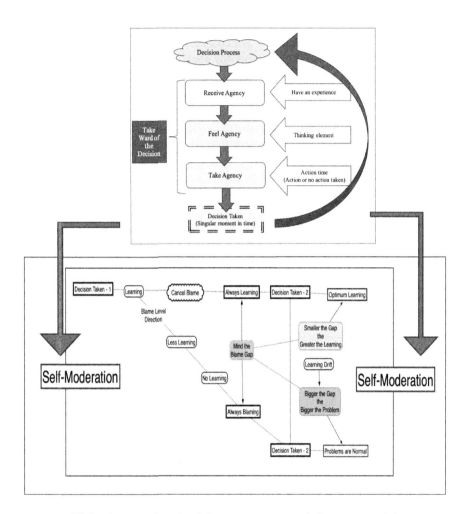

This shows the decision process and the potential
drift between decision (1) and decision (2).

I will now work through the decision process and sit it next to the
compounding of decisions taken and consider the effects of drift in life,
as Scott Snook presented. The top graphic we have the process that has
been explained. Information enters your body from an experience and

the decision-making process begins. Agency is received through the senses and from that the feeling of agency process begins. The battle of your mind takes place through the feeling of agency and ultimately you conclude that process by taking agency and deciding upon an action to take or not take: a decision taken (action or no action). That decision is set in time and is a singular moment in your life. As time goes on, you begin to self-moderate. You either repeat the decision because it works, or the self-moderation process continues because you feel you need to develop that previous decision taken. As Snook intimated, you must keep on top of the decision process across all factors that lead to it and not let it drift from its original position. The standard and quality will be maintained, unless you allow practical drift to occur. As drift occurs from the original decision and complexity increases around the decision, the original reasoning becomes uncoupled. Charles Perrow suggests, if you do not stop that drift, accidents should be expected to occur and are considered a normal consequence. The bigger the gap and drift, the bigger the problem. If you base your decision on a drifting initial decision taken, you now have a virus of negative trajectory in your life, business or organisation.

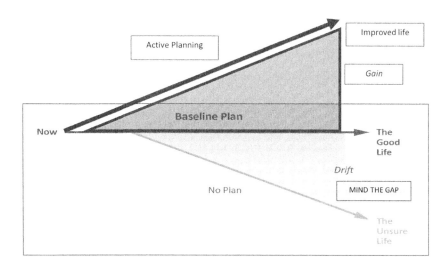

'Mind the Gap': between a good life and an unsure life.

Cancel blame

Cancelling blame from your life lies alongside **Rule 1: Take Responsibility** across everything you do. It also lives within **Rule 2: Control Emotion.**

Blame lives within the *'feeling of agency'* element and is captured within the 'wilful lie'. It involves feeling that someone or something else is responsible or at fault for the decision you took being wrong. To say or think that someone or something else forced you to do something wrong or is responsible for something bad happening is relinquishing your **Rule 1: Take Responsibility.** Cancelling blame means not judging and deliberating over the content of decisions. In the receiving of agency, it is set that you start with nothing at the point of each decision taken. You remove prejudice, previous emotions, motives, attitudes, feelings, from the past and the present, and look at the decision taken without judgement. You also do not look at others, as the decision taken is your sole responsibility. There is no blame to consider as you have cancelled it. This powerful factor helps you to enhance the decision process tenfold and now the positive compounding of good decisions has no boundaries.

What cancelling blame does is improve the sustainability of your decision journey in the future and enhances the compounding of your decisions to a better and good life. If you link the feeling and action of cancelling blame to the meaning you create in life (Rule 3), the critical path you construct to do this will limit the drift away from your life, business or company goal. If you are enjoying what you do and are comfortable in what you have decided to do, you are moving into **Rule 7: Be Confident.** Now the world will become a far better place and you give yourself every chance to achieve the good life. If you can compound decisions as an individual to live and lead the good life, can you imagine how powerful that would be as a team? Now that is mindbogglingly powerful, and the potential of the good it could do is immeasurable.

Rule 5: Good Life Challenge

a. Never let yourself drift. Stay ahead of the curve.

b. Keep compounding decisions effectively towards a good life.

c. Keep compounding your decisions across all your day-to-day activities.

d. Compound your decisions to be positively different.

e. Keep compounding good habits and behaviours for growth and success.

Let these statements flow over you and watch out for your drift danger signs. Emotions and feelings you may have:
Procrastination, boredom, low interest in your environment, lack of drive, lack of determination, lack of direction, lack of belief, no-option feeling, arrogance, ignorance, avoidance, fear of experience, fear of learning, anger, manipulation, distraction, complacency and ego.

And now face the challenge!

Recognise compounding decisions is the end-product of Rules 1 to 4. So, if you take responsibility for all that you do, control your emotions to be constructively positive each day, create meaning in everything you do, and never stop learning, then you are on the trajectory to a good life. So, my challenge to you is to stay ahead of the curve, and compound the positive constructive decisions you make and take on a day-to-day basis. Cancel blame, look into your soul and be ward of your own destiny. When you know or feel things aren't going right, catch yourself by revisiting the first four rules. Don't be a bystander in life. Stand up and become you by compounding great habits and behaviours from the learning you embrace each day. Don't be scared or fearful if you are in a dark place: there is an alternative. Take responsibility to change your direction in life, even if it is simply asking for help, and from that you will start moving up your life curve again. Give yourself moments of good agency, feel the agency within your mind and take agency to grow. DO NOT wilfully lie to yourself as that will cause drift in your life. Rather than wilfully lying, stand back and reflect. Self-moderate to ensure that you stay ahead of the curve on a daily basis and compound those positive feelings and thoughts into great habits and behaviours. The momentum you create from compounding positivity will lead you to the good life you want. It is a great direction to go in, because you give yourself a chance to action **Rule 7: Be Confident** in all you do and enjoy all you do with a smile each day

So, keep compounding decisions effectively. Trust in yourself and the people around you. Keep looking and keep growing your knowledge, skills and experiences to add to that trajectory of gain and improvement. Keep that momentum going, stay ahead of the curve and everything and anything is possible for the good life you desire.

RULE 6
TO A GOOD LIFE:

WORK TOGETHER

Why Do You Need to Work Together?

Working together is better than working apart.

My *7 Rules to a Good Life* should not be seen as linear and can be dealt with in any order (that is why they should not be seen as steps). But it is fair to say that, without the first three rules, the next four rules cannot be properly fulfilled. My first three rules are solely about you, taking responsibility for yourself, controlling the emotion around the responsibility you have taken, and then creating meaning and direction in everything you do. You could say that my next two Rules 4 and 5 are the main body and the engine that drives your good life: never stop learning and, when you do learn or feel something good happening, see it is an improvement and compound those decisions to mould your habits and behaviours into how you want to live day-to-day.

The power of working together is simple. If you embrace Rules 1 to 5 and work on them each day on an individual level, **Rule 6: Working Together** becomes the positive growth of a group (irrespective of size) into a team. This might be in a small group such as a family or it could be a Fortune 500 company. The only difference is scale and size. The key here is not to allow the *7 Rules to a Good Life* to become clouded in complication, as that is when their power diminishes. This will happen if you do not manage **Rule 2: Control Your Emotion** and you allow the battle within the mind from the agency you have received to play tricks in your head.

If you embed the *7 Rules* into each individual person in a group or team, they become a single body living the *7 Rules* as one. This is how successful groups and teams live, from solid families and outstanding sports teams to special forces units, Fortune 500 companies and those attempting to expand areas of human capability. By embracing the power of difference and placing **Rule 1: self-responsibility** at each person's feet within the group, you tap into all the skills, knowledge and experience available, driven by personal motivation, so that every person is working towards a clear common goal that each team member can touch and see for themselves. The big cumulative compounding effect of this is that everyone recognises their important part in the journey to success and fulfilment and knows the 'why and how' of their role within the overall success and good life of the team.

It is a fact that the best teams embrace diversity, celebrate diversity. The best teams respect difference and harmonise that difference. The best teams share responsibility across all levels, as each person in that team clearly knows why they are part of it. A sustainable team is only as good as all its constituent parts working together. In the best teams, all individuals take responsibility towards the common goal, and they control their emotions as they know each one of them has knowledge, skill or experience that will be called up at some point, tapped into as critical to the team's success.

The opposite of working together is increase in risk in the team and ultimately the reduction in quality and level of success of its objectives. As Charles Perrow suggests, you should then expect accidents will be normal. And Scot Snook argued you will drift away from your operational performance and enter the unsure life: so, mind that gap.

If we remove failure from our vocabulary, when things do go wrong the team as a whole needs to simply accept that, when there is something missing within their team, they must recognise that they need to develop some further skill, knowledge or experience to rectify the problem.

It is the same process for you as an individual as it is for a team, in regard to taking responsibility, controlling emotion and creating meaning. When you hit the sweet spot or reach maturity as a team, this is when a team becomes a single body and all the constituent parts are performing at their best. If you look at all successful companies or large organisations, everyone knows why they belong in that team. And when a team acts as one, they are so much more powerful than each person on their own. However, the power is generated from each individual in their particular role taking responsibility for that role. They control the emotion within that role towards other roles around them. They know why they are doing what they do because of the clear meaning set by the team, company or organisation. The bottom line is we are better together than apart. That goes for families, groups of friends, small businesses, large businesses, sports teams, entertainment teams, minor projects, major projects. We are better as a society, a nation and ultimately as a planet.

The result of each individual in a team adopting the *7 Rules to a Good Life* is that this good feeling grows if they work to the same rules and see themselves as one; even to the extent that you can transcend beyond self-actualization as a team. Do not underestimate the powerful potential of compounding decisions as a team working together. Also do not underestimate the destruction that can occur in a team when individuals are not working together, but living in the virus that is full of wilful lies.

So, the *7 Rules to a Good Life* apply not only to all individuals, but also to any team in which individuals strive for and work towards the same goal and meaning. You can take that even further; can you imagine how powerful our planet would be if we worked together rather than fighting each other? Sadly, that is the problem with turning our world society's cultural juggernaut around. So once again I bring in my friend Albert Einstein with a reminder:

Doing the same thing over and over again and expecting different results = INSANITY

—Albert Einstein, possibly

I prefer to say to a group or team:

Doing lots of intelligent, positive, different things to get results = SANITY

—Dave Armstrong

I have been lucky to work in some outstanding teams. My favourite team was during my time in the military. In 1983, after the Falklands War, I was lucky to gain a place on the Royal Navy gymnastic display team[58]. In that team we toured the United Kingdom and a bit of Europe performing two displays: mast-manning and a window ladder scenario.

Standing on the top — Button Boy

Mast-manning involved a team of 32 sailors and a ground team, performing at shows in front of tens of thousands of spectators. All the sailors would enter the mast to music, with the button boy leading the team into the arena. The person at the top was called the button boy because he stood on a disc no bigger than a sailor's hat 97 feet in the air with just a pole to hold on to. The pole was strategically placed behind him so he could salute to the crowd.

Those are my mate Dean Simpson's feet on the button and me on the ground waving, I was next up as the bugger beat me to it first that year. Yep, a bit mad really. But I was lucky to proudly do that in front of friends and family on a few occasions. Although I was lucky to do the main job now and again, as a team, we shared that role between those who were brave enough (some may say stupid enough) to do it. Each time you did the button boy, you descended from the mast on a 120-foot rope (to *Superman* music), hand over hand, directly to the dignitary to collect your medal or gift. Dean and I know for a fact that we could not and would not have survived that high-risk show if we had not worked as a team, from our amazing coaches to all the members of the team and the supporting staff around us, including people at HMS Excellent (a Royal Naval shore base). The same applied to the window ladder display. That was a similar high-risk display where we created patterns as a team in a matrix formation 60 feet in the air. That is me in the photogrpah below in the top box letting go at a night display in Aberdeen in front of my parents (Sorry, Mum and Dad!). Letting go is the big scary moment when you exit the window ladder upside down. The full display is performed to music, and the top four sailors are left in the ladder on the bottom rung after completing a 20-minute patterned show as the big finale. The four of us would each exit the ladder doing a thing that was called the suicide drop to the rumble of a drum concluding in a crashing symbol. That meant hanging upside down on the rope 30 feet in the air, then on cue letting go and dropping down the rope head first, where two of your team members were ready to catch you in case you did not break in time and stop. Now, *that* is trust in your team.

Royal Navy Window Ladder Aberdeen.
Me about to drop, in top picture.

However, the greatest example of that was in a team I applied for but never got in, sadly: the Royal Navy Field Gun Crew.[59] This is by far the single best example of working together I can think of, as the consequences for not working together as a team were severe injury or death. The field gun competition was a history-based competition where three teams, Portsmouth, Devonport and Fleet Air Arm, competed over a series of 'runs' at the Royal Tournament held at Earls Court, London. Each run started in front of the Royal Box. The crews pulled the guns and limbers to the end of the arena where they turned and carried themselves and the equipment over a five-foot wall. The guns and limbers were then dismantled and carried to the top of a ramp on the 'home side' of a 28-foot 'chasm'. The crew would set up a wire and traveller so all eighteen crew members and their equipment could cross the chasm. The team and equipment then passed through a hole in the 'enemy wall' at the end of the arena. Each crew fired three rounds to end their 'Run Out'. The average time for the 'Run Out' was 85 seconds.

Field Gun Grew flying over the chasm

The second part of the competition (the 'Run Back') involved the crews taking all their equipment back over the wall and then back across the chasm. Once all the crew and equipment were back on the home side of the chasm, the wire and traveller were dismantled and three more rounds were fired in a rear-guard action. The average time for the 'Run Back' was 60 seconds.

In the final stage, the 'Run Home', men, guns and limbers passed back through the hole in the home wall and then the teams 'hooked up and pulled for home'. The clock was stopped as the teams crossed back over the start line. The average time for the 'Run Home' was 21 seconds.

The record for the fastest run at the Royal Tournament was set by Devonport in 1999, the competition's final year, with 80.86 seconds for the Run Out, 58.65 seconds for the Run Back and 20.92 seconds for the Run Home, an aggregate of 2 minutes, 40.43 seconds. I should point out here that the total weight of the equipment they ran with is in excess of 2000 lb; that is 143 stones or over 900 kg. The barrel alone was 900 lb which is the weight of an old Mini car. All this weight and equipment was thrown around like a rag doll by a team of eighteen. One mistake or one slip by one person could and did cause injury. What I did not know at the time, although they were right in front of my face, were my *7 Rules to a Good Life*. Even down to my **Rule 7: Be Confident** and enjoy what you do. Every person who joins the Field Gun Crew and Royal Navy Gymnastic display team is an excited and motivated volunteer, and it was quite a competition and an honour just to get on those teams each year, never mind being a member of 'A' crew. Field gun crew slots were so keenly sort that the Royal Navy held elimination tests across the Royal Navy at many locations each year even to get in the squad. I am yet to see a better example of how working together is more effective than working apart within an environment of such high risk to self.

To summarise: working together in positively motivated atmospheres has enormous benefits to a team's development, but also huge benefits to all the individuals in that team with regard to the quality they produce and the risk they remove. They can overcome whatever challenges are placed in front of them due to the fact they work as one body of people.

So, what are the consequences of *not* working together, where risk is increasing and quality is reducing? The Hillsborough football disaster in 1997, the second Manchester bombing 2017[60], the downfall of Carillion in 2018[61], the Grenfell Fire in 2017 and ultimately war in any of its forms. These are all examples of not applying my *7 Rules to a Good Life* at every level and therefore we must recognise, when these problems and disasters happen, we have created, at some point, negative and destructive drift in those events by compounding bad habits and behaviours, with a lot of wilful lying around that. Therefore, accidents should not be a surprise. It is always confusing to me, and should be to you, why we only really learn or change when something tragic happens. It is madness, and totally avoidable if you are proactive in working together as a team right from the start.

At a personal human level, this negative destructive drift working in a team can be seen in marriages, families, friends and jobs.

I repeat: it is the madness and insanity of humans that we wait for things that we can feel will end up with catastrophic and tragic outcomes to happen before the penny drops and reality kicks in. I am not saying I am special or ignorant to these life events that can happen to me too, as indeed they have: left homeless in 2007 and ending up sleeping on Euston station with nowhere to go, yet still serving as a fire officer with Manchester Fire Brigade. At that time, I was not aligned with my teams either personally or in work. On top of this, I had completely lost my way in life in all aspects of my Wheel of a Balanced Life. So, I know from experience that successfully working together is the cumulative compounding effect of the positivity coming from each member of the team.

From those experiences in the Royal Navy, I have never told anyone what to do as their leader. I believe the key role of a leader is to create an environment to succeed towards the targets and goals you have set. All

I have ever done is what was done to me in the military by my leaders: placing responsibility right at the feet of each of my team members, then creating an atmosphere for them to succeed. To me, that is what the role of a team leader is: to create a clear meaning that everyone can buy into, control the emotion around them and place responsibility right at their feet.

The other danger in working together is having too many people who are the same and who blow smoke up each other's arses. The worst comment I have ever heard when putting a team together is that people are put in a team because they are a 'good lad' or 'good girl'. That may be so, but if they cannot do the role to the standard you want for that team, or if they have disjointed loyalty, they will know they are not right for the role. Please manage this wilful lie. Friendliness will quickly go out of the window if you base your work together on the soft emotion of liking the person, and they 'blow smoke up your arse' and say the things you want to hear. Do not be blinded by physical appearance. Make sure each team member takes responsibility for the role required of them. You must all control your emotions to be constructively positive with each other each day to get the job done. Be happy to work towards a shared common goal with meaning that everyone buys in to and is motivated to work towards. Make sure you learn together as a team by sharing knowledge, skills and experiences, and from here the trajectory for you as a team working as one is towards your good life. Appreciate that by developing and compounding good behaviours to form effective habits as a team, through the values, laws and standards you all agree to, you all benefit from the team journey to the good life.

Dr Meredith Belbin[62] explained why certain teams perform better than others: they tend to be more successful when they are made up of a diverse and balanced mix of behaviours. Teams perform best when they celebrate difference and have a diverse set of skills, knowledge or experience to achieve the meaning and goal that has been created. The teams who work best together have constructive debate with respect for all working towards the common goals. Meredith Belbin talked about a suite of team role profiles such as:

Completer/finisher: Most effectively used at the end of a task or project to polish and iron out problems to completion. These team players usually have the highest standards of quality control. They can be seen as a perfectionist, but also as an over-thinker.

Team worker: Those are the engine of a team who get a team to gel. They will carry out the work required and complete it on behalf of the overall team goal.

Specialists: Those are people within a team that have a skill, knowledge set or certain experience that can help a specific task. They can come in and out of a team as and when required.

Plant: These people are needed to create movement towards a goal. Good at solving problems. They are usually free thinkers who can generate ideas and can restart or reboot forward momentum in a team.

Belbin's other roles are: resource allocator, co-ordinator, monitor/evaluator, shaper and implementer. Remember, the beauty of difference is in the complementing diversity around you. When you have that strong diverse mix of talent, everything is possible.

ACTION	SOCIAL	THINKING
Completer finisher	**Co-ordinator**	**Monitor evaluator**
Seen as an introvert who will ensure what you do is completed. Seen as a perfectionist and self-driven. A character that will get you over the line.	Usually, the wise one who brings it all together. Great communicator and sees the value of difference. More aligned to a coaching style and helps teams grow together.	Makes and takes decisions and bases those decisions on facts and through emotionally controlled critical thinking. Great for bringing logic into your life.
Implementer	**Resource investigator**	**Plant**
The organiser of an environment who can bring control and order to a given situation. Generally disciplined and can turn vague ideas into reality. They can be unselfish and work for the good of the team.	The person who looks to ensure how things can be done effectively and who needs to do what. Makes ideas from others come alive. Usually, a positive and effective character who creates structures for success.	Free thinker and creative person who can move something on. Can sow the seeds of new ideas and can be innovative about new solutions to create meaning.

ACTION	SOCIAL	THINKING
Shaper	**Team worker**	**Specialist**
Self-motivated person who tends to be extrovert and can drive new directions. Tends to be positive and thrives under pressure.	Usually, a likeable extrovert who is thoughtful and considerate to others. Will adapt for the team and will offer help to others in need. They are indispensable for the overall result to be achieved.	Deemed as an expert or has a certain skill. A specialist will have in-depth knowledge of a chosen subject. Needs to be managed in a team as they are singularly focussed on one theme.

How Do You Work Together?

Team development has stages you cannot ignore. Not knowing this will lead to confusion, delay and reduction in product quality with an increase in risk.

Tuckman's Theory

There are many models, theories and frameworks out there I could use to explain this, but I have chosen Tuckman. Tuckman's Theory was first proposed by psychologist Bruce Tuckman[63] in 1965, and can be applied to and understood within any group or team (friends, family, work) and highly successful businesses and organisations of all types and sizes. I have taught Tuckman for many years at universities and colleges, and use it to help people see the journey they make both within a team and within themselves. Tuckman provides an explanation of a human behaviour or a felt emotion. There is a beginning, a middle and an end, bit like life really. They are set across five stages: forming, storming, norming, performing and adjourning.

At each stage in the Tuckman process, the framework of agency, will play its part. At each stage, you receive agency through your senses. You may be entering a new team or a new person may enter a team you belong to. From that initial interaction and experience, you move backwards or forwards in the relationship, and any of your senses will let information from the behaviours of team members enter your body. The big one as always is controlling your emotion when you feel the first embers of received agency. Particularly, you need to control your previously formed prejudicial or stereotypical thoughts, feelings and attitudes. When you do that, you will form a true emotional feeling within your mind that is without influence. However, if you allow your prejudgement to taint your thinking, you will create a diluted perception of the person, group or team. Depending on how well you control your emotion with the people in your team, you will then take agency at each stage by making decisions and taking action (or not taking action), whether you move to functioning maturity as a team or move backwards to immaturity and embed a disjointed state in the team. Please note that the ideal path is to move through the five stages gradually with incremental growth as a team; but beware this should not be seen or felt as a purely linear process, going from one stage through to the next stage and so on. The true feeling you have at each stage is the key here. You form the relationships and learning about each other with little or no information or experiences to hand and trust in what you see, hear, feel and touch. Then you seek to challenge and test each other in the storming stage, to see how you gel. From that beginning comes an understanding and expectance of each other and the roles you play in a team, which is when you normalise your relationships. In the final performing stage, you are all working together in harmony as one team with little or no thought required as to how this is working so well.

There is, however, one more stage: the adjourning stage. This is the closure or ending of a team which can be reached in many ways, good and bad. It can also happen at each stage when certain situations occur. Ideally though, you end or adjourn the team when you have reached your goal and intended success. This is the ending of a working mature team in a positive atmosphere of successful conclusion.

Let me delve a little deeper into that team journey and explain each stage for you.

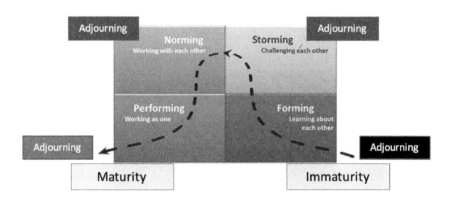

Tuckman's Theory of Team Development

Forming

The first stage of a team or group of people intending to work together, live together or be together is the forming stage. This is when a team or group is introduced to each other for the first time. Generally, people tend to behave independently at this stage, some full on and loud, some calm and unspoken. In this moment there is no understanding of how each one feels and most probably trust will not be given. People are sussing each other out, asking about skills, backgrounds and interests.

What are their goals in life? What do they like or do not like in life? It is important to note here that everyone will participate in this stage, but each person will participate in the forming stage in different ways and at different levels while little is yet known of each person's skills, knowledge and experiences. At this stage, the team or group starts to develop an understanding of the part each person will play in the relationship.

You will notice I have placed adjourning at each stage as this can happen at any time for any reason. Even at the forming stage, some may call it quits here and decide the group or team they are entering is not for them. So, they walk away from the team, thus taking agency in that moment. The decision they make to no longer to be part of that team leads them to take action to leave. The alternative decision to make and action to take would be to stay with the team and enter the storming stage.

Storming

The storming stage is when the mental battle commences between team members. You start testing the others to see if they are the real deal. Can they substantiate their claims to experience or at least show they are genuine by actions and deeds? This is the stage where egos may start to show themselves, and sometimes bullshitters can lay themselves open. Team members may demonstrate calmness and solidness in building relationships by being consistently authentic and honest. Anger may raise its head within the group or team as members disagree on different areas or voice concerns about different aspects the group may need. Feelings of agreement may be discussed within the group or team, as well as areas of similarity. One interesting element to this storming stage is that leadership may arise from different individual behaviours. Common direction may be forming to drive a way forward, or polarised positions may be setting in, which can leave the group in a stagnant moment. If we relate this storming stage to the agency process, this could be described as a team experiencing a moment of receiving agency and then feeling agency.

Norming

So, you have formed opinions, you have stormed through the relationship battles and you now enter the norming stage. In this stage, your relationships are settling down with agreement to go forward. The team or group sets an agreement, formal or informal, to work together or be together. But do not get complacent at any stage as moments of shared new information or action could take you backwards or forwards as a team or group. There may still be some incidents of conflict and you may ride on the cusp of the storming stage again. However, with a feeling of clear direction from shared goals and values within a background of trust, progress can be made. You begin to normalise your relationships. However, particularly in business, that does not mean you need to like each other. You must set clear boundaries, rules and laws that need to be consistently applied. It does help enormously, though, if you can normalise the relationship with a smile in the soul. With this good feeling, you can easily move to stage 4: performing together.

Performing

The performing stage is where your team can hit the sweet spot with a cohesive group dynamic where each team member understands everyone's strengths and weaknesses. You accept your differences in role, behaviour and emotions. You understand that celebrating and embracing the differences within the group or team leads you to outstanding performance. As Abraham Maslow would suggest, you self-actualise as a team or group and therefore can transcend to peak performance with contentment within whatever you do. Each member is embracing **Rule 7 to a Good Life** by being confident and enjoying what they do; confident and motivated in being together. Leadership in this stage is subtle. Some teams or groups will never make it to this stage, but if they embrace the *7 Rules to a Good Life* individually, they will give themselves the best chance to do that as a team. The top teams call this stage *peak-performing*. Fortune 500 companies and highly successful sports and performing teams thrive in this area of Tuckman; you can too. A consequence of performing together is that it can spark new inventions, new ideas, new behaviours of excellence and togetherness. From this point, anything becomes possible and you become what Aristotle calls wise as a team or group. Therefore, you give yourself the chance to deal with the things you know you do not know with ease and a positive acceptance. More importantly, you are open to and accept that there are things out there you do not know you do not know, as yet.

As with Maslow's level of transcendence in life, the performing stage of Tuckman should be every team's ultimate goal in regard to joining up behaviours and thinking. As a planet, our destiny relies on this. Not seeking to achieve this will lead to drift in life and ultimately our destruction. But we are better than that, so let us be sane together: the time to learn is now!

Adjourning

The adjourning stage is the coming to an end of a team or group. In project management, this is now seen as a vital moment to reach and hopefully it is achieved in time and in budget. It was only in 1977 that Bruce Tuckman added this fifth stage to his original framework. Happily, this fifth stage marries Tuckman's framework to the continuous improvement cycle of Plan – Do – Check – Act, commonly known as the PDCA cycle, set by Dr William Deming in the 1950s. The key to reaching this stage is ensuring that it is a happy parting of the ways, as future ventures can be sought from a base line of previous positive experiences and relationships.

The adjourning stage can be accessed at any point of the four stages. Make sure on an individual level that it is a choice you are happy with, as the aftermath of exiting a team in a negative destructive context can cause long-lasting suffering for all involved.

The power of working together

To summarise my **Rule 6: Working Together** and show the power of it, I want to reflect on one of my proudest achievements. Some may not deem it significant, but the environment it was acted out in was significant and powerful. In addition, this experience of mine can be adopted anywhere and at any level by anyone. In 2005 the fire service I worked for had recently (2003) exited a national fire strike. There were on-going battles with senior management and partial performance issues that caused further disruption and hostility. These negative disputes led to pure hatred being aired between senior fire service managers and front-line firefighters. This hostile atmosphere was not conducive to working together as a team. More importantly, it could have had drastic effects on operational performance and safety when attending incidents. I was privileged to be the station commander of a fire station of four talented teams called red, blue, green and white watches.

Eccles Fire & Rescue Station Manchester

The time approached for the station to hold an annual open day for the public in the surrounding area. However, due to the non-compliance attitude of staff, there was no movement by the four watches as they refused to do anything other than attend operational incidents. Good will towards management had completely gone out of the window. Using my skills from the armed forces, learned from officers I had served under, I presented to the four watches a position of reality. I asked them: 'Who are the real sufferers of you not doing an open day?' I got them to remove their anger and I placed responsibility and duty to the community they served right at their feet. And I left it there. No shouting, no ranting nor ordering, only the setting of a moral position.

In the military, I was never told what to do: that is the irony of military service. I experienced what civilians never see. I was presented with the responsibility I had agreed to and the commitment I made during my oath to the Crown. So, when I became a leader outside the Royal Navy, I adopted a similar position; to the extent that I cannot remember ever ordering anyone to do anything or having the need to do so as a leader of a team. All I did on every occasion was place and set responsibility at the feet of my teams and then step back.

One of my Leadership courses at the
National Fire Service College.

I have been fortunate enough to have had many lead positions, most notable as course director at the fire services college in Morton-in-Marsh, UK; as lead researcher during our brigade's modernisation project in 2005; as a national leader on the development of incident command systems, and as officer-in-charge at many incidents, large and small. So, I had a meeting with all twelve watch officers, and asked them that question. Three months later, they ran a fantastic open day with everyone participating and smiling. They managed themselves, lead themselves and completed the open day on time and in budget. More importantly, they started to perform and work together again as a team in a station without anger. I simply created an environment for them to succeed, by laying responsibility at their feet, controlling emotion around the event and creating meaning for them that they were happy to fully engage with.

My first ever fire as officer-in-charge, with a wonderful crew, white watch, in Atherton, Greater Manchester, was a basic car fire. When

I arrived, I jumped out of the left-hand front seat where the officer-in-charge always rides, and as I jumped off my crew were nowhere to be seen. I walked to the rear of the fire engine where they were all stood awaiting orders. I remember looking at them, men of various ages (sadly no women at that time), all with many years of experience under their belts. I asked what they were waiting for. 'What do you want us to do?' came the reply. I looked at the car fire and said, 'orange glow: talented people go'. They asked me to repeat what I had said, which I did, and then said, 'Surely you don't need me to tell you what to do on this?' They went off and put the fire out. After that fire, every incident we attended, I released their abilities from the mental cage they had been kept in. My predecessor had run each incident with over-control which killed personal responsibility, deflated the crews' emotions and demotivated them, leaving them with little trust in their abilities and skills. All I did was release that obvious potential and skill set and married it with trust and belief in themselves. Most of these firefighters had part-time jobs running businesses, leading on charities, or working with people outside their job as a firefighter: I simply tapped into that.

Please do not think I was special. I just adopted the habits and behaviours that were ingrained in me in the Royal Navy at a young age, including my understanding that a team is only as good as all its parts. If a group or team is devoid of meaning, it is dysfunctional and its skills and experiences are never fully used. As I went through my career from joining the fire service in 1986, I was fortunate to work with and under so many amazing firefighters and officers. Wherever I worked Salford, Agecroft, Eccles; it was really only down to some amazing watch officers who released their firefighters' skills to their full potential. They learned from every incident they attended and then compounded those skills over and over again. Those watches where always fun places to work and I am indebted to all the firefighters I served with, both within the team and as their leader.

The sad part for me was that all this was lost outside the watch or station environment. As officers progressed through their ranks to the top jobs, many were more interested in being in power and working towards the big pension pay day than serving the public. They lost focus in their roles, and many selfishly focussed only on progressing their careers. Silo-working was rife, where each area and station worked independently of each other, which is not conducive to working together. If you look at our public services today, the reason we are in a mess and so disjointed is that our social services, from carers of old people and our vulnerable, to the police and our hospitals, do not work together. They have separate budgets with the focus being on 'more for less.' I understand the need for a fiscal policy but we have so many problems today with the full integration of public services, problems of isolated performance with little or no central meaning. The message is confusing from the top: who are they and what are they working towards?

This is why my *7 Rules* have their place at every level, making sure everyone knows and takes responsibility for what they do and get paid for. Within that, they must control their emotions and become emotionally intelligent at all levels: do not let the wilful lie of personal selfishness destroy that. Make sure that at every level you create meaning that is clear. In your strategic documents, ensure you have a joint goal that everyone can see and touch in a practical and physical sense. Ensure everyone has the desire to keep learning because they want to, rather than are told to. Make sure that, when you work as you do, you compound decisions positively and constructively upwards rather than negatively and destructively downwards. The drift you create is the way you go. If you get complacent, you will stop moving forward and you will begin downward drift. Remember: when you realise you are drifting in a downward trend, you can always catch yourself at any point of the curve and start the upward journey again. It is your choice as you receive agency via your senses. Make sure you control the emotions within battle of the brain. Make sure you create a meaning that is achievable for everyone involved. You never know, you might become confident and then enjoy everything you do together: my Rule 7.

Look at the teams you are in. Does everyone know what their responsibility is? Remove anger and set what you are doing in a positive professional environment. Make sure everyone is invested in the team or group by creating meaning that is shared by all, from cleaner to chief executive. Remember what a high-performing team working together is, that all the roles within it are important to the group's or team's strategic jigsaw, and each member recognises each other within that, even if they are performing a different role. Happiness within a team is having shared values and complementary behaviours which lead to team harmony, because what they are doing has value.

Risk in teams is simple; the bigger the gap between strategic thinkers and front-line workers, the bigger the risk, the bigger the crisis and the bigger the fall.

Once you set this atmosphere to succeed by employing **Rule 4: Keep Learning** and **Rule 5: Compound Decisions,** individual and group learning goes through the roof and anything you put your mind to as a team is achievable. Always remember working together is so much more powerful than working apart. This is how you improve and gain in life at all levels, whether you are part of a family or part of an international global company. Sanity therefore is: doing lots of intelligent, positive, different things *together* to get results.

Rule 6: Good Life Challenge

a. Look to continually develop and grow your team each day.

b. Work together with others across all your day-to-day activities.

c. Working together effectively will change your life for the better.

d. Ensure your team has the required behaviours and habits.

e. Ensure your team has the required skills and knowledge.

f. Working effectively together as a team will lead to growth and success in life.

Let these statements flow over you and beware of your drift danger signs. Emotions you may have:

Prejudice, selfishness, stereotyping opinion, dismissive of diversity, low interest in what is round you, lack of drive, lack of direction, lack of belief in others, no-option feeling, arrogance, ignorance, avoidance, fear of experiencing with others, fear of learning together, fear of sharing information, fear of sharing knowledge, fear of sharing experiences, anger, wanting to create an 'us and them', complacency with others and ego.

And now face the challenge

Always work together effectively with friends, family, or in business: no matter the size or scale. Working together is far better than working apart, and from it, amazing things can and will happen. Think about this: if you embrace the first five **Rules to a Good Life** at an individual level, how amazing life would be if you all 'sang from the same page' and lived the rules together; working to the same rules, values and having the same ethics towards a good life as one team. Please manage the wilful lie of bullshit when you feel it. Friendliness will quickly go out of the window when your team is disjointed and results do not come. So, my challenge to you is, do not be blinded by physical appearance. Make sure that everyone you have in the team has value: that they each take responsibility for the role in the team that is required of them, and that they have the skills and knowledge to perform that role. The best teams who work together have constructive debate with respect, with all working towards the common goal. So, I challenge you is stay ahead of the curve as a team, compound positive constructive decisions jointly and make sure you do this on a daily basis. When you know or feel things are not going right within the team, catch yourself by revisiting the first four rules together. Compound your great team habits and behaviours by learning together as one each day. Give your team moments of good agency, feel the agency within each team member's mindset and take agency together to grow. *Do not* wilfully lie to each other. Be honest at all times, as this will prevent team drift in performance. When you do drift as a team, stand back and reflect together. Do not over-react either in success or when things do not go so well.

The momentum you create from working as a team will lead you to the good life you want. It is a great direction to go in and from that point anything is possible. Anything can be achieved if you work hard at it each day, working together.

RULE 7
TO A GOOD LIFE:

BE CONFIDENT
(ENJOY WHAT YOU DO)

Why You Need to Be Confident and Enjoy What You Do

Welcome to the last rule. Well done and thank you for reading this far. You should now feel, if you have embraced Rules 1 to 6, that Rule 7 is a natural flow from them. Rule 7 comes from knowing what you are doing, being confident with your direction in life, working towards a balanced life, learning each day and compounding that learning as days, weeks and months pass. It comes from achieving all this with a calm mind, knowing you are giving your best each day in a positive supportive environment and atmosphere. Remember: **enjoying what you do is so much better than not enjoying what you do.** My idea from the start of the development of my *7 Rules* was to give you a simple, memorable tool that you can draw upon instantly when your mind is being challenged, without having to refer to a book. So, when your mind floats to an unknown or doubtful place: breathe; take responsibility; control your head (emotion) and create some meaning. These are my first three rules.

Let's look at this in a different way. **Rule 1: Take Responsibility, Rule 2: Control Emotion** and **Rule 3: Create Meaning** are the mental foundation to any behavioural change and habit you build.

First three rules are the drivers to a good life

See the first three rules as the *drivers* of a good life. No matter what you do in life, take responsibility for yourself and then make and take choices that create gain in your life rather than allowing yourself to drift. Get your left brain to harmonise with your right brain and build your spiritual intelligence and intellectual capital. Make sure you place yourself in moments where you can receive positive, effective and constructive agency; feel that agency and then take agency towards your good life. If you don't, either nothing happens or you are manipulated by others into relinquishing your responsibility for your actions and decisions. Therefore, control what is going on in your mind and stay calm and strong. Whatever you do, give yourself meaning through a goal or an objective so you can achieve what you want in your good life. These first three rules create momentum and direction in your life. Think about this: you receive agency from feeling hungry. Biologically, if you do not take responsibility for that, you will starve. Conversely, if you eat too much, you put on weight. So, at the moment of hunger, help yourself and set a target to keep to a desired weight, then you will have a goal that allows you to manage and reflect upon your daily choices. From this, you increase your chances to maintain or gain in life on a daily basis. I know this is easier said than done, but my first three rules give you that chance to help yourself; and they can traverse across all levels of life and society.

I have used these rules for many years and they have helped me to remove anger and think through any situation no matter how difficult. You can do that too. Rule 7 grows on top of these first three rules as your confidence builds with the knowledge that you are doing something today that helps a better and happier tomorrow.

Rules 4, 5 and 6 are the engine that drives your good life

Rule 4: Keep Learning. Follow Rule 4 and keep learning and growing each day. Build and maintain that engine of knowledge and skills through the experiences you allow yourself to be open to. Whatever life you want, learn about food, learn about nutrition, learn about your job, career, business, hobby, passion, family and friends. Learn and grow within your Wheel of a Balanced Life. Whatever resonates with you, make sure you support your goal by learning and growing your knowledge.

Rule 5: Compound Decisions naturally follows on from this. See compounding as the **fuel** you put in your mental engine. Once you are moving in your goal's direction, compound your desired behaviours and habits by repeating them. Keep that good fuel going if you know it is doing you good and your life is improving. Keep looking for that knowledge, skill or experience that will help you grow. Do this over and over again, improving as and when required by grasping opportunities when they arise. Many people like being out of their comfort zone as they know true knowledge, growth and learning only comes from feeling frustrated or vulnerable. These moments are the power fuel opportunities that project your good life and the compounding effect of them has enormous benefits to your good life. Any elite athlete or business person will tell you; it is practising the same thing over and over again that drives your future success and happiness. So, keep compounding those decisions. Such compounding will give you the fuel to drive your future good life and help you stay ahead of your life's curve.

Rule 6: Work Together is the icing on the cake. Following this rule, you can share the *7 Rules* with others. Your team or group will showcase the benefits to be had by working with the same values and behaviours as others because you want to rather than need to. The power of Rule 6 comes from respecting difference and embracing the power of diversity. We all have a place and part to play in the tapestry of life. Make sure yours is a good one! When we become one team with a shared focus, anything can be achieved if you want it as a collective.

Think about this: if you are living the first five rules on you own effectively, can you imagine the amazing things that can be achieved if you put lots of people like you together, harmonising and sharing one another's skill sets, knowledge and experience? Anything becomes possible, and you can spread the *7 Rules to a Good Life* to anyone. Prejudice (prejudgment) and stereotyping of others is a virus on our planet that will only lead to our destruction. Can you imagine if we changed the world's narrative from being angry and dismissive of each other to embracing a collective working together? The opportunities and possibilities have no boundaries.

I remember when I became station commander at Eccles fire station, there was a lot of hostility towards different groups, including between the four watches. This was known as 'watch wars'. What I did to get them to work together (unknown to them) was covertly set my *7 Rules* for them all. I encouraged each watch to take responsibility for them-selves, then I created an environment (emotion) and atmosphere that was conducive to all the watches working together. I placed my first rule right at their feet, for them all to 'take responsibility' for who they were and what they did. I encouraged them to cancel blame from the past and deal with the now. Taking responsibility for self, I believe, is the catalyst for all the other rules. From there, the watches designed their own direction, started to tap into each watch's unique skill set and shared it with each other. Once they felt the benefits of working as four watches within the one team goal, they grew as 'Team Eccles' rather than four watches working independently. So, Team Eccles focussed on its overarching goal, to serve the people of Eccles and the Greater Manchester area, rather than being wholly self-focussed and angry with others. That experience and how they evolved is still one of the proudest moments of my fire service life. It concluded in that open day being designed, managed and run by them, not me. All I did was release their potential by creating an atmosphere of possibilities and togetherness around my *7 Rules*.

By embracing the first six rules, you will enjoy what you do and be confident doing it. It is the effective compounding of my six rules that gets people to work the best they can, grow confidence in each other; and enjoy what they do together. Therefore, if you work, live and drive my first six rules, Rule 7 is an organic and natural growth that will build your confidence over time and allow you to enjoy what you do on a daily basis. It is a ghost rule, so to speak, a natural consequence of the first six.

Mark Twain[64], an American writer, humourist, entrepreneur, publisher and lecturer, once said: 40% never happens, 33% is in the past, 10% wrong mental images, 13% is out of your control and only 4% is real.

So, drive and feed that fuel into your mental engine to expand the 4% of reality. Stop stressing, over-thinking and relying on the other 96%. Remember the three sieves (questions) of Socrates and focus on what is 'true, good and necessary' when you speak to yourself and others. Confucius[65], a Chinese philosopher and politician, suggested.I hear and I forget, I see and I remember, I do and I understand, by recognising these wise words you reduce and remove the virus of hearsay, gossip and tittle-tattle that can and will cause drift in your life.

So, embrace all your senses and do things rather than talk about doing things. Remember the Law of Causality (cause and effect) whereby it is what you do that counts, not what you say you do. Once you begin to grow in confidence regarding your reality, you can use Rule 5 and keep compounding those decisions and building those good habits and behaviours that lead you to a good life.

The Bystander Effect
I want to return to the work of Professor Philip Zimbardo and Stanley Milgram and how humans like to make life easy by conforming to and obeying others and becoming bystanders to the lives around them, including their own. If you do this, you will never get to the point that you enjoy what you do. There will always be, in the background, the feelings of doubt, dread and worry. And, as Scott Snook's work suggests, you have a choice to drift or gain in life, recognising that if you drift, as Charles Perrow concludes, accidents will be normal and should be expected at some point. So, stop being a bystander in your life. Live your life to the full now. You only get one go at it, so stay ahead of your life's curve.

The Parable of the Cave
I would now like to bring the Greek philosopher Socrates and Plato's[66] brother Glaucon[67] into the equation with their **'Parable of the Cave'** This parable was explained in writing by Plato as there are few to no notes from Socrates' and Glaucon's teachings.

The 'Parable of the Cave'

Socrates tells us about people who lived chained in a cave as prisoners from their birth and therefore the only life they knew was within that cave. The only agency they received came from the darkness and from shadows that flickered on the cave's rear wall before them, cast by the fires burning behind them. This cave was the place of their only known existence. Their so called reality within that cave was created by puppeteers in control of their lives. What they were allowed to see, hear, feel and smell was orchestrated by the puppeteers who cast shadows from the fire onto the wall in front of them. The only reality the prisoners could use to make their decisions in life were formed from these shadows, and the feelings generated from them were the only experiences they could call upon.

Remember Viktor Frankl who used the power of his brain to survive the Holocaust? His cave was a concentration death camp forced upon him, but his attitude of not accepting that forced reality allowed him not to be beaten mentally. He released himself from his imprisoning cave by presenting to his mind simple positive psychological tools and frameworks that helped him be the person he wanted to be. He changed the dark and negative forced narrative of his life to one which he had control over within his mind. But, unlike the people portrayed in the Parable of the Cave, he had his past life outside the concentration camp to call upon to form his mental reality away from the forced reality.

On a few occasions, I have allowed myself to live a life I did not really like. The best example of this was when I ended up on Euston station with my life collapsing around me. Yes, the people around me had become my puppeteers and created false shadows in my mind. But, in the back of my mind, I always believed life must be different from this. I was being dragged into the toxicity and manipulations of those trying to get me to conform to their agenda. I am not going to criticise their lives or question their reasoning. They believed those values and behaviours were right for them, for whatever reason and for whatever personal motivation. But what I could do was recognise that those values did not live in my world. So, I broke my mental chains by stepping aside from all that. My first port of call mentally was recognising that the world I was allowing myself to live in was my choice, my decision and my responsibility. So, I cancelled my blame of all around me, looked deep into my soul and accepted that, for me to break free of this cave I was living in, I had to take full responsibility for myself. These were my first steps to living a good life and I had to leave that cave to take them. Therefore, it is up to you, *no one else*, to choose if you want to live in a cave prison or break free from those chains and live a good life for yourself, whatever that means to you.

However, do not think, when you do break free and begin to see what you really want to see, that others will follow. Returning to the Parable of the Cave, I want to tell you about the prisoners who broke free.

One day, one of them breaks away from the chains and creeps out of the cave into the light. This is when he first sees the real world for himself without influence. He can now feel the sun on his face, the breeze in his hair, smell the grass and hear birds and bees around him. He is now using all his senses and the agency he is receiving from these new experiences enters his body from *all* his senses, not just those controlled by others. He gradually understands that he can freely walk left or right, and he can run, skip and dance without restraints. He slowly realises that whatever he wants to do now is in his own hands; the responsibility for his own happiness is now in his hands. After these enlightening feelings of freedom, he decides to let the other prisoners know what it is like to break free of one's chains. But when the prisoner returns to the cave to tell the others how good and real the world is outside, the remaining prisoners do not believe it. Enlightenment is a hard position in life for most to reach as people are scared of their own life shadows.

Enlightenment is a state of awakened understanding of yourself; being confident in yourself and being happy with yourself (without arrogance). It was described by Abraham Maslow as the transcendence from suffering to spiritual liberation. To be enlightened is to be freed from the tyranny of the mind and to experience deep spiritual peace, presence and wholeness. Take responsibility for yourself, increase the 4% of reality around you, and life will be so different.

If we return to the concept of agency: for those who are chained in the cave, agency is received from the shadows controlled and created by the puppeteers. The prisoners can only use sight, smell and sound to receive agency. The puppeteer's control what the prisoners see and hear. They are the agency-givers and controllers of the prisoners. The puppeteers are imposing limitations on the extent to which the prisoners can feel agency.

Now replace the shadows created by the puppeteers in the cave with modern-day television screens in every house, with social media, with radio news and daily newspapers. We rely on such information as our only source of influence at our peril. Do not dismiss the power of this. Look at the example of what happened in the Rwandan genocide[68] where thousands died. People killed their neighbours, adults and children, simply because they were from a different tribe. This genocide occurred over only a few months in 1994, during the Rwandan Civil War. During this period of around 100 days, members of the Tutsi minority ethnic group were killed by armed Hutus. An estimated 600,000 Tutsi died within that short period. The 'cave' of genocide was created by a single radio station: Radio Télévision Libre des Milles Collines. This radio station was the powerful weapon used to incite and direct the Rwandan genocide. It took brave people to break out from the controlling chains of that genocide to tell people on the outside what was going on inside Rwanda.

Interestingly, when people address and then escape from their cave, initially they are blinded by the light outside. The new experience is all too much and trust in this new world takes time. This is why people who have worked hard in their lives, and focussed solely on that work, struggle in retirement: the cave they lived in is gone, and the new world they enter is strange.

However, when you allow all your senses to be open without external control, you can start to base your decisions on grounded and valid thoughts, feelings and emotions from what you hear, see, taste, smell and touch.

Glastonbury Pyramid stage and a poignant message.

I am amazed whenever I take a friend to the Glastonbury music and arts festival[69] for the first time that they can struggle with what they see, hear, touch, taste and smell. They might stand in amazement at this sensory overload, and any preconceived views and thoughts of what the festival entails fly out of the window. Up to this moment, many have deemed it mad, bad and far from their normal lives. But I am yet to find anyone who is not sucked into the true reality and beauty of Glastonbury, which is happiness, togetherness and a celebration of the diversity of life in all its forms. But you need to see and hear that for yourself. Do not rely only on my word: I want you to live your life through your own eyes, not mine. Hold criticism until you have experienced something for yourself. Otherwise, you must accept you could be living in a mental cave, influenced and manipulated by others. Educate yourself for the life you really want through physical experience.

Anyone who has entered degree-level education will know that it is integrity, honesty, and authenticity that gets you a first-class undergraduate degree, Masters or PhD. The information you gather to prove your points is researched with authenticity and you are required to show that what you have written is reliable and has validity. You must demonstrate that you can control the information entering your work via the agency you receive from your senses, framed by your methodology (the research environment you create and the research methods you choose). Once you have proved this, you need to show you can control your emotions around the information you generate, to create a clear meaning from it. That is why triangulation in research is important. You must ensure the agency you receive from the data you collect is taken from three different positions of the argument, giving you the best chance to participate in the 'feeling of agency' process from the information you have collected. You can then 'take agency', present decisions and choices from all you have researched and written, and include them in your conclusions and recommendations.

Remember: you will lead a false life if you allow yourself to create and enter a cave that is based on hearsay, tittle-tattle and gossip. If you do not understand that the cave is merely an illusion, you can and will be controlled by other people, and consequently you will not educate yourself towards an alternative life. According to Zimbardo, Milgram and Asche, conformity and blind obedience will happen if you do not control them.

As the prisoners in the Parable of the Cave are chained, they are unable to use all their senses to the full. They cannot turn their bodies, so they can see only what is in front of them: the back wall of the cave. Plato explains, 'the truth will be nothing but shadows of their images.' Many people live like this because they fear change, which as we know is the only constant of life. People tend to keep to what they know, limiting their experiences and therefore crushing the potential of any agency they might receive. We become the puppeteers of our own lives, and place chains on our life experiences by letting ourselves see only what we think we should see, compounding our self-limiting beliefs, habits and behaviours.

Once again reflecting upon the prisoner who leaves then returns to the cave: when the prisoner goes outside and sees for the first time unrestricted, the world becomes more real in regard to the opportunities available. But many cannot deal with the raw honesty and authenticity of life, so they return to their cave voluntarily, and are happy to be chained up again. However, if you accept that life has differences and you celebrate diversity by receiving agency from your experiences of seeing, smelling, hearing, tasting and touching, then you have a chance to see the real you and the real life around you. And the earlier in life you do this, the better.

Socrates talks about the prisoner who went out of the cave, saw the light and became a philosopher for himself. This is what is known as being in an enlightened state; you have given meaning to your life. Each time I think of the phrase 'the meaning of life' I want to re-watch the Monty Python film *The Meaning of Life*[70]. It is so clever and, each time I watch it, it makes so much more sense and becomes so much more real. The key, if you choose to move to an enlightened level, is to share your personal journey with others so they too can have a chance to open their own 'gateway to learning' for themselves. I am not saying that becoming enlightened is an easy journey: it is not. But, when you give yourself only half of your life story, there is a good chance you may never reach the point where you are happy with simply being you. You are allowing yourself to see only what you want to see rather than letting yourself be open to all opportunities to grow, learn and develop your behaviours and habits for the better you.

Let us take this one step further. The big danger of having lots of people living in the shadows of an unenlightened world is they begin to believe their own shadows in life. They begin to make their own reality by creating their own laws and values from a chained state. They make decisions and take actions that suit themselves only. Adolf Hitler did this on a massive scale, as has every despot in history. He presented shadows of a disjointed reality. It was one massive cave he created, and people followed him blindly or through fear. They followed a reality based upon the creation of a false illusion, that was driven by a toxic and destructive meaning and lay on a foundation of lies full of prejudices.

WARNING

Media and social media are now the puppeteers of your future: watch with caution.

People become what they think they are through the eyes of others; that is a dangerous place to go. The peddlers of celebrity culture are puppeteers of the modern day, promoting perfection in looks and life. This is a false reality for most of us and does not relate to the lives we live, but somehow people get sucked into it. Remember, you may become what they think you are. A lazy-thinking person will be aware only of what exists around them. They will not look outside that cave of life and therefore can be easily manipulated by others. The problem starts when you make yourself a prisoner to a cliché, doctrine, ideology or group whose reality becomes your reality; their cave becomes your cave. Remember, if you never see beyond and get trapped in the shadows of your current life, you are living in a restricted cave. Think of the young gangsters and drug dealers in your area: they know only one way because of the people around them. They are living a toxic, angry, dangerous and unstainable life surrounded by fear, cheating and lying. They are motivated in the short term by quick fixes and high-stakes false reward. They will escape that cave only by being killed on the streets or, if they are lucky, by being handed down a long jail sentence. A better way for them to break their chains is to leave that cave through the power within themselves, rather than being forced out.

The same situation arises for people who are suicidal or depressed: they are chained up in a cave of the mind. Please know that there is always a better option to one of darkness and fear, and if you can get out of that cave, life is so much better. I will give you this poem to think about. It changed my life when it was given to me by a lovely person, Nancy Buckland, who counselled me at the fire service college. I will forever be indebted to her. She gave me the poem at the conclusion of our time together. I hope it helps you too. It is written by Portia Nelson[71], an American popular singer, songwriter, actress and author.

There's a Hole in My Sidewalk: The Romance of Self-Discovery.

Portia Nelson 1920 - 2001

I walk down the street. There is a deep hole in the sidewalk. I fall in. I am lost. I am helpless. It isn't my fault. It takes forever to find a way out.

I walk down the same street. There is a deep hole in the sidewalk. I pretend I don't see it. I fall in again. I can't believe I am in this same place. But it isn't my fault. It still takes a long time to get out.

I walk down the same street. There is a deep hole in the sidewalk. I see it is there. I fall in...it's a habit...but my eyes are open. I know where I am. It is my fault. I get out immediately.

I walk down the same street. There is a deep hole in the sidewalk. I walk around it.

I walk down a different street.

Trust me, if you walk down a different street, dreams can become a reality. Dreams can come true if you work hard at it mentally and physically. All you need to do is break those chains. As Socrates states,

'*You know the things you know*', so form good behaviours and habits through living a good life. Accept that you can always learn; accept that you will have feelings of agency around *the things you know you don't know*, so embrace those life opportunities to grow. Accept that you do not know everything and there are things out there that you cannot even think about. Therefore, accept there are things *you don't know you don't know*. By accepting this wise and enlightened mental position, there is a chance you may one day get to see them.

In the United Kingdom there is a saying 'keeping up with the Joneses' which describes the urge to attain the same achievements, or better, than your neighbours. It is a sort of jealousy or oneupmanship. Remember, each person lives their own life; their life is not yours. They live in their reality, not yours. They live in their cave, not yours. So, build that confidence and break the chains of that process and learn to live in your own light and your own reality as this is the only one that should matter to you. The cave you live in is a limited reflection of your reality: break away from that cave, live and show your full potential. An enlightened state comes when you break those chains and live in a reality where all your senses can fully function. Remember that generally 4% of what you think is real. You need to increase that percentage to move towards an enlightened state.

The next challenge is who you choose to tap into once you have broken free of your cave.

WARNING

Choose carefully the people you let influence you. If you do not choose carefully, you can create an even deeper cave. On the other hand, if you tap into authentic, honest people who embrace similar values and laws to you, then anything is possible. Remember Rule 6: Working Together is better than working apart. Once you realise the world is in fact a beautiful place to be in, you simply need to find the right shore to land on.

One of my passions is music, and it has helped me across many aspects of my life. I am so delighted to land each year on the 'shores' of two music festivals where I work. They are the world-famous Glastonbury Festival in Somerset, England, which I touched upon earlier, and the Green Man Festival near Crickhowell, a town near Abergavenny in Powys, Wales. At these two beautiful festivals, I can tap into a world full of music and performing arts of all types and, more importantly, a world full of my *7 Rules*. Both events celebrate diversity and difference to the full. No one looks down on anyone else, irrespective of where they may come from. You can live there and be there without judgement or prejudice. I can hear a reader saying: 'that's not what I am told a festival is'; I bet that reader has never been to a festival and that judgement comes from what they see on television or stories from people who have been to other, less happy and celebratory festivals.

The singer Howard Jones[72] has kindly given permission for me to use his powerful lyrics to *New Song* that I believe encapsulate the Parable of the Cave. It is a song that may help you as it did me early in life:

New Song

I've been waiting for so long
To come here now and sing this song
Don't be fooled by what you see
Don't be fooled by what you hear, whoa

This is a song to all of my friends
They take the challenge to their hearts
Challenging preconceived ideas
Saying goodbye to long standing fears

Don't crack up
Bend your brain
See both sides
Throw off your mental chains

Don't crack up
Bend your brain
See both sides
Throw off your mental chains

I don't wanna be hip and cool
I don't wanna play by the rules
Not under the thumb of the cynical few
Or laden down by the doom crew.

Don't crack up
Bend your brain
See both sides

Throw off your mental chains

Don't crack up
Bend your brain
See both sides
Throw off your mental chains

I've been waiting for so long
To come here now and sing this song
Don't be fooled by what you see
Don't be fooled by what you hear

This is a song to all of my friends
They take the challenge to their hearts
Challenging preconceived ideas
Saying goodbye to long standing fears

Don't crack up
Bend your brain
See both sides
Throw off your mental chains

—Howard Jones

Now I want you to reflect once again upon the philosophy of Bruce Lee. Bruce Lee was a Hong Kongese American martial artist and philosopher who urged us to *'Be like water'*, meaning we should be formless. When Bruce Lee says to be *'formless'*, in my view he means we should not allow ourselves to be trapped in a certain mindset, in a cave. Instead, we should be able to adapt to situations, grow, and change, and adopt the qualities of water. That's the basic interpretation of the phrase, but there is deeper meaning to be found in it, which can be more easily understood when looking at Lee's background and his previous comments about water.

Look at it this way: water, when it enters any vessel of whatever size, from a cup to an ocean floor, will take the form and shape of the vessel it is contained in. In a settled and calm state, it becomes the area it is contained in; it becomes the shape of what it lies in. Become water in yourself and become the calm you, the best you, the happy you and the enlightened you. However, life is full of peaks and troughs, opportunities and challenges. Be aware that, if the container leaks or breaks or is hit by an outside force, the calm shape becomes angry to the extent that water has the ability to breach any vessel, to run away from the original shape and be changed or lost for ever. You too are like water: you either become the best of you or you do not. You must choose the right vessel to live in and keep calm. I know what I choose.

How to enjoy what you do and build confidence

I cannot reiterate this enough: to start enjoying your life, remove anger from all you do. Stop anger from entering your life as it only creates more anger and causes stress. Anger creates drift in life and, at some point, this has to stop and take a different direction if you want to live a good and happy life. Stop being negative. Change the narrative to a positively constructive one. I do not say be positive only, because positivity does not have as much influence long term if it is not also constructive and has a meaning set towards who you want to be and where you want to go.

Remember the process of 'agency' has a compounding effect on your habits and behaviours, so lose the anger and negative thoughts, lose the doubt and fearful feelings and replace them with happiness, positivity, belief and confidence. Do not drift in life. Reverse the drift and make sure you gain. To work towards an improved life, move away from the unsure life. Have that good life you always wanted.

Become your own lighthouse by keeping the learning light on and scanning the surrounding area. The beauty of this, once you start enjoying being you across all that you do, is that you can be a lighthouse for others. You can start enjoying what you do by changing the narrative and philosophy of your life to a positive one, one that has meaning and direction, one where you can be confident. Keep a look out for your life's risks and do not allow them to become issues.

This idea is encapsulated in a poem by Dorothy Law Nolte[73], an American writer and family counsellor. Her poem *Children Learn What They Live* changes the narrative (story) from a negative to a positive position regarding how we teach children. The poem can be applied to any event in life and any situation: you only need to change the focus. I strongly suggest you look it up. Along with Portia Nelson's poem *Walk Down a Different Sidewalk: the Romance of Discovery* previously referenced, Nolte's poem inspired me to write a poem that encapsulates all my **7 Rules** and presents the flow of agency: give agency, feel agency and take agency.

Poem to a Good Life

Stage 1
I walk into a room.
I feel a dread,
Yet I walk further in.
I feel frightened and fearful,
But I am in.
Now all I want is to get out?

Stage 2
Again I see the entrance to the room.
I feel the same fear and dread,
Yet still I walk in,
Pretending it will be different.

I can't believe nothing has changed.
It's their fault I walked in, they made me.
It takes me a long time to get out

Stage 3
I see the room once again.
I know I shouldn't go in.
But I still do. It's a habit.
I start to open my mind.
I should not be in here feeling like this.

I know it is up to me now to get out.
I leave immediately.

Stage 4
I see the room in the distance.
I can hear the noise coming from it.
I open the door and see the same people in there.
I now know it is not good for me to go in.
I close the door and walk away.

Stage 5
I walk into a different room.
A room full of support, not control.
A room full of hope, not dread.
A room full of love, not fear.
I walk into rooms that lead me to a Good Life.

Beware of the experiences and agency moments you give yourself. Take responsibility, control your emotion and give your life meaning by walking into a different room. Make sure it is the right room for your good life: choose wisely.

Understanding mindfulness

Another way to enjoy what you do is to think about the positive things you can do to change the narrative in your mind. This is mindfulness. It is mindfulness that gives you a chance to grow your confidence towards living a good life. It is taking time out through mindfulness that allows you to reset, realign and reassess why you are where you are and gives you a chance to 'go again'. More importantly, it allows you to build and maintain a positive trajectory to a good life.

The technique requires you to find a safe place to sit back, think freely and relax. When you do get stuck in the world of stress, it is hard to enjoy what you do or focus on the task in hand, so you do not really appreciate what is going on around you. You create a mental tunnel from which you can see life only in one focussed direction. You lose your peripheral vision which results in a constricted tunnel-like field of vision. 'Target fixation' is when you focus on only one thing and you get obsessed with that one thing, preventing you looking outside to what you genuinely feel and think. Target fixation can be seen when an individual becomes so focussed on an object or situation that they inadvertently increase their risk of colliding with that object or situation. Target fixation hides the other things that are happening around you, allowing unseen risks to become issues.

I am not saying that being focussed is wrong. Being focussed does have great benefits in a positively directed world full of hope and ambition, and it can lead to a happier, good life. But please recognise that being obsessively focussed on something you know is not for you and you are not truly happy with, is not healthy in the long run, either physically or mentally. You become blind to what you could do differently. You are forming your own cave in a false reality through the compounding of wilful lies. So, break those chains. This is where mindfulness can help, as it allows you to minimise tunnel vision and target fixation. It allows you to be the safe lighthouse of your own destiny.

For this to happen, you need to do something that allows you to breathe so you can reflect, rethink, readjust and go again. Mindfulness is a great tool to collect your thoughts. The more you practise mindfulness, the more powerful and accessible it becomes. Mindfulness can help you enjoy life more and understand yourself better, and that helps you towards the good life.

So, here are the steps to a mindfulness moment. You can use these steps to develop your mindfulness technique in your own life. Mindfulness involves paying attention to and being focussed on a moment in your life, both physically and mentally. All the tools mentioned in this book, like the Wheel of a Balanced Life and Driving Peak Performance, need you to create focussed moments. Mindfulness ensures you think through, assess and then inform yourself of the true reality of the moment, based on your personal honesty and integrity to yourself. This then allows you to create meaning which is positive and constructive to help you lead a good life. It is easy to stop noticing the world around us. As the Greek philosopher Epictetus[74] tells us:

'The chief task in life is simply this:
to identify and separate matters so that I can
say clearly to myself which are the externals not
under my control, and which have to do with the
choices I actually control.

Where then do I look for good and evil?
Not to uncontrollable externals, but within
myself to the choices that are my own...'

Mindfulness is the basic human skill to be fully present with yourself physically and mentally, being aware of where you are in that moment and giving yourself a chance to feel what you are doing in that moment. Like a peak performer, bring calmness into your life and be happy in the zone by not allowing what is going on around you to overwhelm you. Mindfulness is not a trick or a fad; it is a readily available mental skill and tool you already possess. You first need to accept it is something you can use and then you must learn how to access it. So here are a few tips.

Mindfulness technique and practice

1) **Take a seat**: Find a place to sit that feels safe, calm and quiet for you to relax. This can be anywhere, in any situation and at any time of the day. Even great athletes about to run or swim in the race of their life will access mindfulness on the track or around the pool to become focussed on what they are doing right now. Some people need to be in a room on their own, some people just need to sit down and find a space that they can relax and think privately. Find a place where you can relax, think and breathe quietly.

2) **Set a time limit**: If you are just beginning with mindfulness, it can be like when you first go into the gym: do not do too much or you will put yourself off. Learn the skill gradually by giving yourself enough time to get into a relaxed position. At first, try five or ten minutes. There is no set time your session should last: just give yourself enough time to get into the zone. NB: if you say you have not got the time, then you are wilfully lying to yourself. If you have not got time for this, the compounding effect of your 'I am busy' attitude is not healthy in any form. So set aside the best time and get to that relaxed place.

3) **Notice your body**: The key then is to zone in on your body, bringing your physical and mental sides together, so that you notice and become aware of both aspects of being a human. By noticing your body, you will be harmonising your left and right brain, your chimp and your human brain. This allows your computer, your spiritual brain, to draw information in a calm state. How you stop your mind fighting once

you find your calm place is to sit still in a chair with your feet on the floor. If you want to take off your shoes and ground yourself, then do so. Make yourself comfortable so you can notice your body. Some who practise yoga and Buddhism may take up the lotus position. The key is to make sure you are in a position that you can maintain for a while and allow your mind to take over your body. Introduce your mind to your toes, feet, then legs. Slowly move up the body and focus on each part in turn until you reach you head. And lastly, go into you mind.

4) Feel your breath. Once in a settled position, concentrate and start to control your breathing. Slow your body down and more so your mind. You can do this by focussing on your breathing. Breathe in and breathe out, then start to slow down the breathing to a pace that relaxes you. Sometimes I use music. A particular piece I use is *Clair de Lune* (Moonlight) by French composer Claude Debussy. This beautiful piano piece allows you to wander freely and safely mentally. It is also great in a group mindfulness session, and I use it my coaching course. So just relax and breathe.

5) Keep focussed but relaxed. Once settled, let your mind wander as you breathe. Your mind will leave the focus on breathing and wander to other places. Whenever this happens, return your attention to focus on the breathing. Empty your mind and just relax. The key here is to focus on you, and to control your mind to let yourself do that.

6) Be kind to your wandering mind. Do not judge yourself or obsess over the content of the thoughts you find yourself lost in. Just come back to the breathing. Keep removing the tension from your mind. Over time that skill will develop. If you have negative thoughts, stop them, banish them from your mind and relax again to the breathing. Make sure you allow yourself time to reach this relaxed place and stop your mind wandering. It is important to keep practising mindfulness as, when you get good at this, you can do it anywhere, at any time and in any situation.

7) **Close with calmness.** When you are ready, come out of the relaxed state you find yourself in. Gently lift your head. If your eyes are closed, open them. Take a moment and notice any sounds around you. Notice how your body feels right now. Notice your thoughts and emotions now: they should be more relatable and more noticeable. Your mind should now be able to think clearly and honestly without negative energy.

So don't procrastinate: choose an area from your Wheel of a Balanced Life to focus on and use the Mindstorming tool we learned about earlier to be positively productive. End with a mindfulness session to reground yourself and you will now look at the area in a more balanced and true way.

The other trick is just do the Mindfulness session to get you to a relaxed state, then go again. At first, I did not like mindfulness or take it seriously. However, once I understood the power of it, it was like a breath of fresh air. I find that when I write my books it is after a mindfulness moment that I have my best ideas and most profound thoughts.

The greatest mindfulness session I have ever experienced involved the helicopter in the photograph below and its pilot. The jockey (pilot) of our unit in the Falklands War was surrounded with madness and led a highly stressed life risking sorties (jobs) of all kinds. Sometimes our Wessex V commando helicopters would even go behind enemy lines. So, the background of fear was always there, but in war you get accustomed to the madness, and it slowly becomes your reality. What the jockeys did for their moments of mindfulness was, now and again, take themselves off with us in the back. They would find a convenient rock, lower the helicopter to it, balance the back wheel on the outcrop, then rock up and down in a very calming manner to relax. Most people would see this as lunacy; to the jockeys, and for us in the back, it was how they gave themselves moments of mindfulness away from the madness of war. It is up to you to find your mindfulness safe place. If the jockeys of our unit could do it in the middle of war, it shows it can be done anywhere. So, find your happy safe place and choose your place to be mindful wisely. Mine is walking on Formby beach with my dog Dora. What is yours? If you have not yet got one, go and seek it. Remember: mindfulness regenerates your mind and realigns it to a positive emotional state.

A pilot, a Wessex helicopter, a convenient
rock and a mindfulness moment.

So be confident and enjoy what you do across all your life. If you are in the lows of life or feel immersed in darkness, find your starting point to refresh, realign and reboot to live a good life again. For peak performers there is no excuse: keep positive, stay positive and stay focussed. Live every day to be the best you can be and bloody enjoy it. And if you are not enjoying it, change the narrative and your life's trajectory to a positive one. So, be confident, enjoy what you do and keep smiling! Grab your life now. By taking responsibility for all *7 Rules*, they become yours: you will never regret adopting them. Your future will be yours once and forever.

7: Good Life Challenge

a. Keep out of the caves – if you find yourself in one, break your chains.

b. Keep growing that smile for life!

c. Be confident in what you do.

d. Embrace the *7 rules to a good life*.

e. If you feel you are drifting, regrow and reset that confidence in what you do.

And now face the challenge!

I started this book saying there are two certainties in life, you are born and you die. The uncertainty is the middle bit. The unknown is when it will end. I think we would all like to live a good life. Whatever your vision of a good life may be, its origins are formed within your mind and soul. So, get to know how your brain works.

The big question is: are you living the good life now? If not, when will it happen and how can you make it happen? It will happen once you are confident this is the life you really want and you engage in it with a smile. So, be confident and enjoy all you do. Enjoy the responsibility you take across all your life. Control your emotions and battles of the mind. You know where you are going from the meaning you have created. Every day, tap into agency-*receiving* moments of experience and *feel* that agency so you can *take* agency to live a good and happy life. No wilfully lying to yourself. Banish failure from your mind. Opening the gateway to learning in your mind, through developing new skills, knowledge or experiences is the key to a good life. Once you are happy with a behaviour, skill or habit that you know can lead you to the good life, keep compounding those decisions you take to always keep growing.

Know that, when you do feel drift in life, you are confident that you can catch yourself and keep yourself ahead of life's curve and stay out of those potential dark caves. Be realistic with yourself, and know you may still have bad or down days, but be confident that, through these rules and the meaning you have created across your Wheel of a Balanced Life, you can pick yourself up and 'go again.' Be happy and confident that, with the right people around you, whether that be in your personal or work life, enjoying your journey together is far better than being on you own. Work together effectively with others whoever they may be: friends, family, business colleagues, work teams, no matter the size or scale.

Do not be blinded by physical appearance or false image. Recognise the beauty of life is that we are all uniquely different and you are beautiful in your own right. It is the beauty you see in yourself that gives you confidence. So, keep controlling your emotions to be constructively positive every day and get each job done within your Wheel of a Balanced Life. Become spiritually enlightened and build both your intellectual capacity and human capital. Make sure your Yin complements your Yang. Never get complacent or arrogant with your journey to a good life. Know that from order can come chaos or from chaos order. Make sure you are always happy to work towards your goals and any shared goals you have with others. Be happy and confident about the benefits to be gained by sharing your knowledge, skills and experiences with others, but recognise it is still the responsibility of others to find their good life for themselves. You can only offer your hand: it is up to them to take it.

What advice would you give to your younger self now? This profound question can give you an insight into your future by being honest and learning from the past you. As Einstein (may have) stated: insanity is doing the same thing over and over again and expecting different results. I suggest you change that narrative in your mind and focus on the idea that doing lots of intelligent, positive, different things to get results is where sanity lies.

From now on, love being you, be confident being you and celebrate being you. Embrace each day to be the best and happiest you can be, as you are an integral part of life's jigsaw and it is the sum of each day that makes your life whole. Every piece of what you do each day is needed to make that amazing life portrait of you. The younger you are the more profound these *7 Rules* will be on your life, if you grasp them now. The time to live the good life is *now*!

Embrace your good life now through living the *7 Rules to a Good Life*: there are no excuses. Beware of your wilful lies, manage you caves, break your chains, move towards the light and keep that light burning. Make sure what you feed your brain is true, good and necessary and you will be amazed at what you are capable of. **Don't let your life risks becomes issues. Be 'on point' for you own life. Embrace my *7 Rules* and let them become yours.** Remember, the power and beauty of life is in the differences between us, but with a common bond and meaning, everything is possible and the good life is available to all. **Go and live a good life now. The time to live your good life is now.**

Thank you.
The End

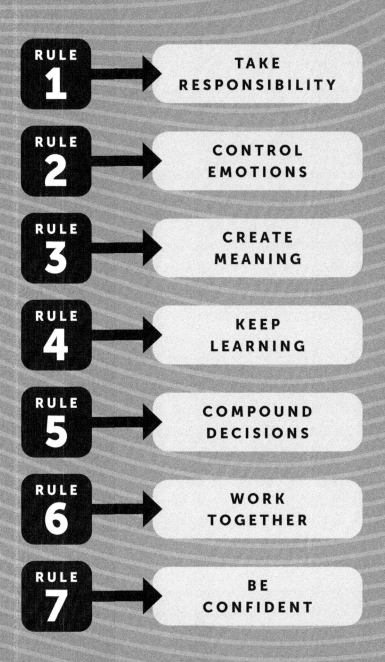

THE PEOPLE BEHIND MY
7 RULES JOURNEY

I WANT TO GIVE YOU AN INSIGHT into how and why I have been able to write this book. The people I am about to introduce to you have been my life's drivers, benchmarks and inspiration. They have taught me to live life, celebrate life and not mourn life. These are their stories.

Four people were the real motivators for me to write this book: you will meet three of them in a moment; the fourth, I'll tell you about in the next chapter. I owe all of them so much. This book is inspired by their stories and their legacy is the *7 Rules to a Good Life*: a gift, I hope, for you as it has been for me.

Brian (Budgie) Marsden[75]

Brian 'Budgie' Marsden

Budgie was my best mate within a group of best mates When I left home at 17, my first draft job/ when I joined the Royal Navy was on the crew of HMS Invincible[76], a brand-new aircraft carrier. That is where I met Budgie as we both worked on the flight deck team as crash firefighters and aircraft handlers involved in aircraft movements (sea king helicopters and harrier jump jets) on and off the ship.

'Budgie' on a flight deck tractor

The bond I created with that team still stays with me today, particularly my bond with Budgie who was a beautifully, happily mad and honest person; a pleasure to be with and a great laugh. Until the January of 1982, we spent many happy hours of fun, working hard and playing hard. Unknown to me at the time, this was the place where I started to feel and touch my 7 *Rules to a Good Life*.

Working on the flight deck of an aircraft carrier is one of the most dangerous jobs in the world as fighter planes and helicopters launch and take off with you only metres away. So, as a team, you have to work together: not doing so is not an option as people could get injured or killed. The aircraft were either flying, in the hangar (the garage) below or chained up on the flight deck and ready for deployment. When the engines were turned off, the sea harriers were held secure on the flight deck by a series of chains that were shackled to a variety of ring bolts set in the deck. This secured the harrier from moving while at sea. In addition, as salt water would spray constantly over the deck, the intakes of their engines would be blocked by a sort of wooden blank cap to protect them from the elements. This blank cap was pushed into the opening by means of a metal pole sticking out of it. Sadly, as is often the way with amazing major designs, the storage of these blank caps was missed in the design of the ship. However, there was a guard rail that ran around the island of the flight deck that was just wide enough for these blank caps when not in use, to be stored with the wooden cap against the bulkhead (wall), which left the metal pole sticking out from the wall. From 1979 on, all fight deck staff had experiences of the poles catching them, sometimes very painfully, on the body as they passed them. I was no exception.

We complained many times that these poles would cause serious injury. We even joked that one day they would kill someone. But, compared to the other dangers of a helicopter bouncing off the deck or a sea harrier landing, a single pole sticking out seemed a minuscule risk. So, for years, until I left to join my junglie (commando) helicopter unit in January 1982, these incidents with the blank cap poles continued. I left HMS Invincible and Budgie stayed on, and he ended up working on the flight deck throughout the Falklands War. The war ended on the 14 June 1982, after 649 Argentinian military personnel and 255 British military personnel had died.

So, the war ended and, on the day after, a force 12 storm greeted the peace. For ships this is a problem and HMS Invincible was no different. The ship was getting thrown about but, as the war had only just finished, it was prudent to have a few aircraft ready for quick deployment if required. So, a sea king helicopter was turned off ready for deployment on one of the take-off spots. After a while it began rocking on its chains. The storm had freed the chains slightly, and they needed tightening up for fear of losing the helicopter overboard. So, two volunteers were asked to go out into the storm and tighten the chains on the sea king. Budgie, of course, volunteered and off he went out into the storm, successfully tightening the chains. However, to get there and back was easier said than done in a force 12 storm, and part of the route involved holding tightly to the island guard rail to make your way back to the rest room. As Budgie made his way back, the ship hit a big wave and caused one of the tractors that weighed quite a few tonnes to slide across the deck. You may appreciate that, in a force 12, hearing is not a sense you can rely on. So, Budgie never heard the tractor coming towards him. It pinned him to the bulkhead, crushing him against it. His crew members then worked frantically to get the tractor off him, which they did. But Budgie still hung there. One of the blank cap metal poles had pierced his body, causing fatal injuries. As had been predicted since 1979. The team cut him free, but the medics couldn't save him. He passed away and was eventually given a burial at sea.

This all happened the day after the ceasefire was set. For the people left behind, you can imagine the effect of the guilt at not having dealt with the pole risk earlier. Budgie never leaves my mind to this day, and I still harbour guilt for not being stronger in raising the risk of injury when it arose in the first instance. As soon as he died, bespoke storage units were built on every ship in the Royal Navy to store the blank caps correctly and safely. For me, this has been and always will be a profound moment. From it, I will always feel guilt at not doing something when I knew the risk was raised, but it has also ensured I never forget the lesson this experience gave me. It is my moral duty to Budgie to embrace it and remember it in my future life.

That was my first experience of an accident or incident that, with hindsight of the injury and death caused, could so easily have been avoided. It was my first experience of the compounding effect of a risk ignored developing into a tragic foreseen issue. It raised, for the first time, my thoughts around why humans have to wait and get to this stage of incident, accident and disaster before we do something about it. One of the reasons I have been resilient throughout my life is I have lived my life for and with Budgie next to me, as he can't and I can live a good life. I too had many near-death misses during my time in the Falklands and it was through this experience of war that the penny dropped regarding how precious time is and how quickly life can be taken away. By the grace of God, I survived. At the tender age of 20, my first lesson in life was: never get complacent about how lucky you are to be alive, fit and healthy.

To Budgie, I owe everything. It was his death that sparked my understanding and appreciation of my *7 Rules to a Good Life.*

Paul Metcalfe[77]

Paul Metcalfe

Paul Metcalfe was an outstanding operational officer. He was a leader (commander) of small- to medium-sized incidents, and the fire service at the time didn't take seriously the teaching of command skills and associated required behaviours for running incidents as the lead person. The training was nothing like the quality I was used to in the military, but the fire service adopted what they thought was good practice.

However, in 1999 I designed a new command course to give people incident command skills and knowledge which included a test of their behaviours away from an incident. Paul was programmed to attend my course later in the year. Tragically, before he could attend, he was requested to attend a water incident on the 5 September 1999 where it was confirmed a man had disappeared under a stretch of water that was metres deep. At the time, the fire service was not recognised locally, nor nationally, to deal with such incidents. So, appropriate training was not forthcoming and the correct equipment for such incidents was not made available to use. Like on many occasions, the heroes, the firefighters, would turn up and do their best with the equipment that was available. For many years and from many people across the UK, concerns were raised about the dangers of firefighters attending water incidents, with near-misses occurring regularly, intimating the potential for an operational tragedy.

Paul travelled to the scene and on arrival he was given the information that the person had disappeared and had been submerged for over an hour in water metres deep. In the cold light of day, with time to think, we all know, as did Paul on route to the incident, that the person is possibly dead and this may be a job for divers to retrieve the body. But when you have not had emotional assessment and are not trained in command behaviours, you never learn that the hardest decision at an incident is to say *no* and do nothing as there is no life to save. There is nothing to be done as the person is dead, and it is a diving team's job to retrieve the body.

The fatal mistake Paul made was to get sucked into the crowd's demand to do something or be seen to do something, with the added pressure from other emergency services around him including the police and their helicopter flying above. Don't get me wrong: if there had been any chance that the missing person might still be alive, what Paul did was what all firefighters would have done: made an effort with what they had on the fire engine to rescue that person. Paul was one of us who worked day-to-day on the front line of fire and rescue. However, the raw fact was the man in the water was dead by then and it was the divers' job to get the body out.

Sadly, Paul succumbed to the crowd and the situation, and it was that pressure that caused him to show willing. He decided to appease the crowd by getting a rope off the fire engine, an old general-purpose line, and tying it around his waist. He began to swim out to the place where the person had disappeared under the water. After a while, due to the cold water, Paul started to struggle, so his crew began to pull him back to dry land. But the line was not fit for purpose and most of its length sank under water. Unknown to Paul and his crew, the line had attached itself to a tree under the water and this is what pulled Paul under. The many brave attempts by his crew members to help him were in vain. Paul died at the scene.

I must emphasise that Paul and his crew did what we would have all done at that time, because the mental training of command was not available as it had been to me in the military. But the many requests not only for such training but also for the right equipment to be given to firefighters to deal with such incidents went ignored or were avoided for many years. On Paul's death, the magic money tree came out and firefighters in the UK were prevented for attending such incidents for a while. All firefighters were ordered to attend new water rescue courses. New equipment was bought and training in water rescue made available. Equipment such as throw ropes, floatable rescue ropes and life jackets were purchased rapidly for all fire crews. The response to Paul's death went even further as UK-wide dedicated water rescues teams with rescue water craft were formed. What angers me, and should anger you, is why it takes a death for something to change when the questions were already being aired and should have been addressed earlier.

It was the compounding effect of ignorance and avoidance of a known risk by senior officials in the fire service that was a major factor in Paul's death. Those officials were supposed to lead and manage such known risks to avoid a tragedy.

Strangely, as I write this in October 2022, the findings of the inquiry into the second Manchester bombing in 2017 are being broadcast live. The same ignorance and avoidance of previous risk is highlighted, with the chief officer of all emergency services apologising to the general public for gross mistakes being made and stating that lessons will be learned. If I had a pound for every time, I've heard that, I would be a rich person. The problems are not solved by putting a band aid on the risks now and saying sorry. The real cultural issue is how you stop the compounding of risks in regard to known risks being ignored or avoided in the first instance and then allowing them to become major life issues.

Paul's was a tragedy that could have been avoided. The greater the communication gap between front-line staff and strategic policy-makers, the greater the risk and chance of an accident occurring. So, at 36, another major lesson landed in my life: when you see a risk in its first instance don't let it be ignored or avoided. To Paul I will be eternally indebted for this experience, and I don't want his avoidable and tragic death to be for nothing. Paul was the catalyst for all my rules, in particular **Rule 4: Keep Learning, Rule 5: Compound Decisions** from that learning, and **Rule 6: Work Together**. Unfortunately, the authoritarian and hierarchal approach in emergency services can increase risk due to front-line staff been so far apart from the senior strategists who make decisions and lead policy.

I was asked soon after Paul's death if he had attended the command course; he had not. I was asked on numerous occasions, was I sure he had not attended my new command course? I repeated, 'no, he did not, sadly.' I was then ordered to say that he had. I refused, and my journey to Euston station began. If I had signed a letter saying he had attended, knowing full well he hadn't, how disrespectful and insulting to Paul, his family, and his team would that have been? And how dangerous to the safety of future firefighters that would have been, as the compounding of ignorance and avoidance would have continued. Plus, it would have broken my moral code embedded in me by my parents and through my military time, and would have been totally disrespecting Paul's legacy.

Paul made my *7 Rules* come alive and I will be forever grateful to him. I only hope his tragedy can help others in the future to keep learning in life and compounding those decisions to ensure they live a good and safe life.

You might be questioning why I include these stories, and in particular why they are so raw. I believe I owe it to Paul, the crew who attended with him, and Budgie, to ensure their stories are told so their deaths can help others in a positive way to live a good life. I also hope that the stories of their deaths can help prevent unnecessary deaths in the future, or at least reduce the risk of them. I could not have written this book without my experience of Paul and Budgie. Rest in peace, both of you.

An unknown Argentinian soldier

Navy Point, our home in 1982 - Stanley across
the way — View from our helicopter

War is the ultimate compounding of negative and destructive wilful lies. This came shockingly to my knowledge at the tender age of 19 when I came upon an unknown Argentinian soldier after the Falklands War had concluded. Part of my job was to check the area behind our garrison home known as 'Navy Point' directly across from Port Stanley, the capital of the Falklands. Our home was a disused cow shed that sheltered our tents. Behind us was a rocky hill that housed the Rapier anti-aircraft missile battery that protected the entrance to Stanley from enemy aircraft. One day during our wanders around the craggy rocks, we came across a foxhole in an open area of land. It wasn't the traditional short rectangular box with a cover of grass that you can hide in, but a rise in the land and the entrance was the side of that rise.

As we ventured carefully towards it, we noticed a body inside. It was that of a young Argentinian soldier. The horror and trauma of our discovery was that he looked barely 16 years of age. It was evident he had been so scared, he hadn't ventured out of his foxhole. He seemed either to have had a head injury or he'd died of hypothermia. What was even more horrific was that his head was half eaten by maggots from what looked like a small calf that he must have grabbed hold of as it passed the entrance of his foxhole and was using as food. It seemed to me he was a very young conscript and my profound torturous thoughts was: 'what were he and I doing there?' The image of that scene stays with me today. He was just a kid, and so was I.

The craggy hilltop with the Rapier battery

That moment was the beginning of my mission to remove anger from my mind and body, and it was in that moment I became a defensive pacifist (like many war veterans do). This means I remove anger from my soul and celebrate and respect the difference of others but will defend my difference if bullied. Prejudice, anger, greed and power-grabs cause more prejudice, anger, greed and power-grabs. It's the ultimate compounding effect from the horrors of war. So, I questioned why I and the young Argentinian were even there: he was no different from me. What was I doing there with him in the midst of this manipulated madness? You can come to me with every excuse in the world to justify war, but it remains the end 'agency' moment of the ultimate compounding of negative and destructive energy and wilful lies. Someone has to break the chain of anger to move forward, so why get angry in the first place? Hence, I created **Rule 2: Control Your Emotion.** Why don't we change the narrative of any war story in the first instance, to work together rather than working apart (Rule 6)?

My experience with the young Argentinian soldier set me on the path to create the *7 Rules to a Good Life*. I owe so much to him.

So, I am eternally and sadly grateful to Paul, Budgie and the unknown Argentinian soldier, and it is to them I dedicate my book. Reflect upon their lives and consider yours. Out of respect to them and many more like them, who have risked their lives on your behalf, embrace your life and keep going with a smile, or go again if you're struggling. What a legacy you leave for them, if you allow them to influence your happiness and good life.

THE TWIST IN THE TALE: THE ONE LIFE RISK MOST PEOPLE WANT TO AVOID

THE GOOD NEWS is the good life is here if you want it.

But here's a new thought: it is learning about and your understanding of *death*, respecting it and not being overawed by or frightened of it, that can lead you to a true good life. This, along with liking and even loving who you are, are hard for many humans to come to terms with. I say to you, embrace who you are and know you are beautiful in your own unique way. Then build your good life from that.

History is littered with examples of avoidance and ignorance of potentially fatal risks (known and unknown) in all areas of our lives. Look at how you think about your health, fitness, happiness, relationships, work relations, business relations and how you view yourself and your self-esteem.

However, the subject of death is the risk in your life that many are uncomfortable even to think about, never mind talk about. Particularly when you're young and feel you are 'bomb-proof' from danger, you think death is so far away. Yes, that is maybe the case, but don't forget you can't buy back time and I can tell you, at nearly 62, time runs away from you without you even knowing. That's why the question 'what would you say to your younger self?' is such a powerful one. I suggest you ask yourself this question every five years at least. It allows you to think and self-moderate intelligently and go again. Also don't let any personal Wheel of a Balanced Life risks grow to become issues. Again, the good news is within the *7 Rules*, as all it takes is for you to change the narrative in your head to a positively constructive one.

Death comes in all its forms; the lucky ones get to live a full life into their late 80s and 90s. Life expectancy is now around 80 in the UK, that number varying around the world. Even that risk of people living longer with no provision for the support mechanisms required in older age has been ignored for too long and lack of social care is now a major issue in the UK. However, many die earlier in life. The big illness issues are obesity, stress, heart disease and cancer. I bet many of us never thought of Covid being tossed into this equation only three years ago. This is raw for me as my mum died of Covid on 1 November 2020. She was 82 and had had a great life with my dad; and my brother and me, of course.

The beauty is that there is always an alternative; there is always a different approach to consider, and you can play your part now. Take responsibility for your life and death now, controlling your emotions around death, and create meaning for your future direction and life. Always keep learning about what you can do today to help your better tomorrow. Set yourself up for a regret-free and happy death. This can be achieved by positively compounding every decision around your Wheel of a Balanced Life, by building your spiritual intelligence and growing your intellectual capital. Take control of your brain and compound good habits and behaviours along your life's journey. Do not underestimate the compounding effect of each one of us reaching for enlightenment, and stop being a bystander in your own life. Recognise that the life you lead doesn't have to be a lonely one or an unhappy one. Recognise that working together is greater than working apart and that the celebration of our differences is key. Choose your family, friends, colleagues and fellow adventurers carefully as you journey through your life. Be authentically confident in what you do and enjoy what you do with a smile each day, as it is the sum of all the constituent parts that makes your whole life story towards your final days. I will say it again: it is understanding death, respecting death and not being overawed by or frightened of death, that can lead you to a true good life. All it takes is to find out who you are and what you want to be.

NICKY'S INSPIRATIONAL STORY: LAST DEDICATION

I WANT TO END THIS BOOK with my last dedication and place before you a personal story that we can all relate to. I hope it will help you understand why it is important to change your attitude to life and death to a positive one and reduce your fear of death so you can live a good life. I urge you to respect and embrace the fact of death; then, once you have, put it to one side in your mind and enjoy life. Reflect upon this story and use it in whatever way you want, as long as you use it in a positive way.

I want to be open about this as I believe having an insight into the inspirational woman, I was fortunate to share my life with can help you in living a good life now.

I was blessed to have a woman in my life called Nicky who became my wife in December 2013. I met Nicky a few years before that when I wasn't looking. I had decided I was crap at relationships, so took responsibility for my life and decided I was going to live life on my own. This was not because of the other people in my life, but because of me, regarding my doubt and self-worth. Something was always missing with the relationships I had, and they all seemed to go wrong. I was looking in the wrong places and at the wrong people. I needed to walk down a different relationship street to find out who I really was and who I really wanted to be.

My wife Nicky

Nicky changed my life. She was totally different from the people I'd had relationships with before. She was a magnificent fine artist in glass and her temperament was set around art and music. She was born in Burnley, but lived her life in Wrexham, North Wales. However, it was after she had lived a troubled abusive childhood, and not so happy early adulthood, that we met. I was completely amazed by her attitude as she had every excuse to be angry, but she didn't even know what the word meant. Her outlook on life was beautiful, gentle, thoughtful and kind, even after her traumatic upbringing. Nicky's key saying on everything she did was 'it will be rit (right)'. No matter what she faced.

I thought of her as a beautiful flower in bloom every day, nothing was a problem, and every day was fun. She embraced a good life every day.

However, after Nicky forced the issue three times about a rash on her nipple, the doctors succumbed to her and she had a biopsy in early 2012. A few days later we were called into the hospital and the conversation took place that most of us dread. 'Nicky, you have cancer in the right breast.' After that bombshell was dropped on our laps, the doctor continued, 'The good news is, if we can do a mastectomy, there is a great chance you will live a longer life.' The shock comment was, 'The operation is next Friday'. The ground seemed to open and this massive void of nothingness welled up in my head. As we walked along the corridor silently, just holding hands, I turned to Nicky and asked how she was. She replied, 'It will be rit'. I am not saying she wasn't frightened or sad, but the way she acted and behaved from that day forward was a privilege to observe and be part of. Life got more real, fun and focussed on just 'being' and enjoying each day. Nicky went back to work, and we continued our life as normal. Weeks after the operation, we were called in to the hospital where Nicky was told, 'The cancer is now not detectable, but there may be rogue cells'. Her chemotherapy commenced soon after, and, three years later, she was given the all-clear and told she could have reconstructive surgery.

As you would expect, we started to restructure our life to the one we wanted, and Nicky and I began the move to Liverpool after her reconstruction. Life was great and back on track, and even happier. I know many readers who have been through this will understand the euphoria of an all-clear.

The reconstruction commenced in 2015. The surgeon was a beautiful man and talked Nicky and I through the procedure. As it was around the heart we talked about the known risk. Once again Nicky said, 'It will be rit'. The operation went ahead, and we began to celebrate life again. A week after the operation we were sitting in the alcove of a local pub having some food. Nicky's phone was on the table, and it began to ring. The screen said, 'Doctor Hospital'. For some reason we both knew what it was and reluctantly Nicky answered the phone. The doctor told us they had found scar tissue during the operation and it was malignant. This was the day the world turned upside down; for Nicky and everyone close to her. I wanted the world to swallow me up. That was the only time I saw Nicky's face drop in all this time; she was human, after all. So, we shrugged ourselves down and went into the hospital that evening.

At the meeting on 22 April 2016, Nicky was told the cancer had returned in her bones, liver and lungs and that the situation was now incurable. The oncologist was reluctant to use the 'T' (terminal) word but informed Nicky that, with further chemotherapy treatment, she could have three to eighteen months of life. She was still only in her mid-forties. She decided not to go down the chemotherapy route but took an alternative option, using cannabis oil. She knew it wouldn't cure her, but it did give her a more relaxed environment and chance to live a good life until it ended. So, we set up our end-of-life adventures. We went to our favourite place, Corralejo in Fuerteventura, and we went with her children and family on days out. We went on many walks in the Lake District and Wales with our beloved dog Dora, a black rescue Greyhound (who many know as the fastest couch potatoes in the world, due to the amount of sprinting and sleeping they do). We made sure whatever we did was fun, happy and good. Two months before her death, we went on a hot air balloon ride with Nicky's daughter Daisy, and her best friend Tracy and her daughter Lilly. So, even in this dark time, we still led a good life, a happy life.

Hot Air Balloon Ride — October 2017

Nicky and I took responsibility for the situation we were in, controlled our emotions around the inevitable and gave each day a meaning until the end. Beautifully, Nicky also shared her cancer journey with others on a weekly Facebook page, showing warts and all to help others. From how to use cannabis as a relaxant, to treatments and procedures in hospital, and her journey through first diagnosis. She gave meaning to her shortened life through a profound and unselfish goal: helping others.

Something Nicky said in her final week resonated with me around my thinking about my emerging seven rules. She was lying in her bed in the wonderful hospice Queens Court in Southport, and she turned to me. 'When I die don't let two people die. I will be dead, but you are not. Please don't die mentally. Live your life to the full for me, but more importantly for yourself, and enjoy every day with a smile. Remember, life is for the living not the dying. Please live your life to the full, but don't be on your own. If you find another special person to share your journey, grab that too.'

Truthfully, I wasn't interested in another. I was quite happy to take Nicky's love with me to the grave. But amazingly I was introduced to Anna and her wonderful son Matthew in 2018. In August 2021, Anna and I, together with two good friends, poured Nicky's ashes into a hole to settle within the roots of the King's Oak (Druid's Oak) Tree that stands proudly within the stone circle area of the Glastonbury music festival site in Pilton. She did say plant a tree and let that be my place of rest. Now that tree is known to me and her friends and family as Nicky's Tree.

Kings Oak Stone Circle Area Glastonbury (Pilton) —
Anna my soulmate left, Elaine and Bill our good friends
with my ugly mug front. Red roses indicate the hole
via which Nicky's ashes were sent into the tree

The reason I have told you Nicky's story is that it is something all of us can relate to. So *please learn from it.* That is what Nicky would have wanted. In fact, this isn't just Nicky's story as there are so many people out there who have had the same journey; whether that be through adversity like Budgie and Paul or through illness like Nicky. Some, like me during the Falklands War, have survived (thankfully).

Some, like Nicky, were not so lucky. But we have all seen the rawness of an unexpected death. I sense those people and the people around them who have had this experience shouting at you right now:

'Go and find your good life and, when you do, grab it with both hands.'

Please begin to live your good life from this moment forward. There are no excuses. Change the narrative in your mind and keep that gateway of life and learning open, even if you pick just one thing a day to do or take responsibility if you find you can't cope and recognise you need the help. At one point in my life, this was about simply getting out of bed, as I couldn't see the point. So, pick yourself up, be as good as you can be each day, be happy with what you choose to do, then just do it.

Nicky's story should show you it is the wrong time to start to live your good life when you get phone calls like she did in 2012. Life is for the living, and you are responsible for that. Nicky lived a good life every day, even through the dark times. Her story, along with Budgie's and Paul's, teaches us to celebrate life now and be the best we can be each day for a better tomorrow.

The real power within these stories is that the younger you do this in life, the more opportunities you can create, through the experiences you give yourself, to live and compound that good life now. Regarding the younger generation: this world of ours is now yours. So, grab your good life now. Recognise that what you do now can have a powerful and motivational effect on others around you because of the happy and confident example you set. If you look after yourself, you are better placed to look after others. Please spread the 'positive viruses' of my *7 Rules* and make them become yours.

Dora the family Greyhound

One unexpected sad note as I write these last words. On 10 July 2023, Dora our beloved dog had a heart attack and died when running freely in a park. No pain: just dropped to the floor. She was ten. Once again life tests me and bites me on the bum unexpectedly. But I dust myself down and go again. The people before me (and Dora) can't, but I can. This is the least I can do: to respect their deaths by living my life with them in my heart and soul.

FINAL THANK YOU

TO ALL MY FRIENDS AND FAMILY, a massive hug to you all. I am honoured that you allow me into your lives (cue abuse from my mate Ste).

To my parents: thank you for giving me and my brother a great foundation to life. To my beautiful wife Nicky, who passed away far too soon, and her children Joe and Daisy: thank you for renewing my hope in life and giving me the belief to become me. To my brother Mark (yes, you are my world... sorry) and his partner Matthew who have supported me so much.

To all the teams I was fortunate to work with in the military: you gave me the pathway and the foundation to create my *7 Rules to a Good Life*. To all philosophers, academics and people who push the boundaries of life and our existence: thank you. All I have done is put your work into a simple seven rule structure that anyone can use irrespective of background and education. To all my students: thank you, as you have taught me so much in the responses you gave to your assignments and dissertations. To the staff and students at the fire service college: thank you for sowing the seeds in me to help others live their lives to the best of their abilities through the power of coaching. To all my front-line colleagues in the fire stations: your bravery and excellence in serving others by putting your lives on the line each day have been an inspiration to me throughout my fire career.

Thanks to Jed Simpson, son of the famous Simo (had to get that in, lol): your narration on the audiobook is awesome. Thanks to Greg Veryard for his studio magic to make my audiobook come alive. To Victoria, my internal designer, thank you for bringing form and light into my book. To all my beta readers I am internally indebted. To J, my editor: massive thank you. My book would not have come to market without your magic. (Get ready for my next book.) And to my lovely Southport Writers' Circle: thank you for your candour and support.

To Simo and Andy: thank you for giving me access to some amazing professionals and my link back to military expertise over many years. To Mike and Gill Bitcon: thank you for believing in me and being my mentors in life. My time with you both was so precious to me during my career in the fire and rescue service. To all the people in music and the arts, particularly at Glastonbury and Green Man Festivals: thank you for creating spaces in this world where my *7 Rules* come alive in bucketloads.

To my children, Joe, Neve and Mason: I love you all and always will.

To Budgie, Paul and the unknown Argentinian soldier, I will forever be indebted and I hope I do your legacy in life justice.

To my partner-in-crime, soulmate and best friend Anna, and her awesome son Matthew (my gift in life, as he is for everyone he meets), not forgetting our beautiful Greyhound Dora (RIP): thank you. It is down to you that I now know I will leave this world with love, a smile and without regrets.

Finally, if you are reading to this: thank you. I am humbled you have taken the time to read this far. Please make these *7 Rules to a Good Life* come alive for you now. You won't regret it.

You have all helped me choose the right time to live a good life... phew. I am indebted to you. Big hug to you all. And breathe.

APPENDIX

7 Rules to a Good Life
- *7 Rules to a Good Life* (book).
- *7 Rules to a Good Life* (Audible)
- *7 Rules to Good Life* (Kindle)
- 'A **video tutorial** on my Live Life Smarter YouTube channel.
- https://www.youtube.com/channel/ UCuW2WRY9Qkmf_9JhFSV1ByA

What next? Live Life Smarter Programme
Now you know the *7 Rules to a Good Life*, here is what is available in my **Live Life Smarter** coaching programme which accompanies this book to develop your good behaviours and habits across whatever you do.

The five key modules are based on the foundations of the *7 Rules*.

1. Smarter You
2. Smarter Teamwork
3. Smarter Management
4. Smarter Leadership
5. Smarter Business

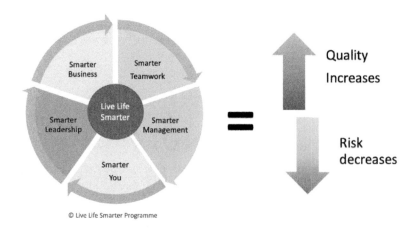

© Live Life Smarter Programme

Live Life Smarter coaching programme

- Five focussed **Live Life Smarter** coaching areas A to E: a rolling programme across 35 coaching units.
- A 15-to-20-minute video tutorial on my **Live Life Smarter** YouTube channel to support each coaching unit
- An optional open forum 2-hour live interactive coaching session on Zoom on a single themed coaching unit or focussed area from across the 35 units.

Each module contains seven coaching units. That is 35 coaching units over the full **Live Life Smarter** coaching programme which I run via Zoom or face-to-face. Each module allows you to tap into your preferred learning style, be that aural, visual, or kinaesthetic (watching, reading, listening and doing).

Each unit has six key parts:

1. A set single focus area presents you with frameworks, doctrines, models and tools for you to design your own life, work, business habits and behaviours.
2. Simple explanation of that area to set the scene.
3. The WHY: various supporting models, frameworks and stories to encourage you and direct you to research and coach yourself.
4. The HOW: variety of models, frameworks and stories (sometimes my own) to help you see what you can do for yourself. This is supported by a variety of inspirational quotes that encourage and help you to visualise your own world.
5. An affirmation exercise: this sets the positive direction and drive for your thoughts and behaviours.
6. Coaching challenges.

Total Flexibility

The **Live Life Smarter** Coaching Programme is totally flexible and is led by you in every way: a true coaching experience. You can read or listen to the manual *7 Rules to a Good Life* and/or watch the videos, thereby coaching yourself, researching for yourself, without direct input from a coach. However, if you want to add that personal experience, you can attend a two-hour interactive coaching session in a group format.

The Aim and Drive Behind the Coaching Programme

The drive for the programme is to reduce your life risks and increase the quality in everything you do: whether that be developing a relationship, helping your children, supporting your friends, working with others, managing a project, leading a business or becoming an elite sportsperson or artist. The general principles of the **Live Life Smarter** coaching programme flow through all these areas.

Use this **Live Life Smarter** programme to get the best out of every day. Recognise that anything you wish for in your life can be achieved. This is the essence of the **Live Life Smarter** programme. The beauty of life is we are all different and it is that tapestry of life that makes us whole.

Being happy has always been my goal and counterpoint in life – what is yours? This **Live Life Smarter** programme will help you set and develop your life pathway. Grab your life now and take responsibility for it. You will never regret it and your future will be yours forever.

BIBLIOGRAPHY

THE SECRET TO LEARNING is in the doing and exploring, so I have set up this bibliography with notes to act as a research starter for you. Read the references and explore for yourself. It is for you to investigate what resonates with you and to build up your own depth of knowledge. Take responsibility for your own research, control your mind and emotions, and give yourself meaning within your research.

Nothing I have written or presented here has not been said or thought about before; from Aristotle, Socrates, Plato, Epicurus, Zeneca, to Einstein, Frankl, Freud, Adler, Newton, Darwin, Aurelius, Mandela, King, Nietzsche, Locke, Maslow, Deming, Zimbardo, Asche, Milgram, Peters (Steve and Tom), Hawkins (Stephen and David), Covey, Haden, Grint, Bennis, Goleman, Handy, Sinek, Peterson, Rohn, Robbins, Drucker and Kolb. Sadly, philosophy from female thinkers has been much ignored, neglected and disrespected, except for the likes of Hypatia, Heloise d'Argenteuil, Tulia d'Aragona, Bassi, Eliot, Arendt, Rand, Beauvoir and Murdoch. However, the new and growing female perspective will have profound effects on our future thinking which up to now has been predominantly from a male point of view. That glass ceiling needs to be smashed to smithereens.

If you read the work of all these thinkers, you would not need me, as my *7 Rules to a Good Life* come from them. It has taken me a lifetime to research and what resonated with me were the common themes flowing through all their thinking that helped me to develop my own. I recognised that most people would never think of reading to the extent required to see this linkage. Plus, many philosophers and scientists present their work in academic terms and have academic debates that only confuse us ordinary folk. I have designed my rules to be simple and to live in your mind so you can recall them in an instant.

For biographical notes, I have referenced the *Oxford Classic Dictionary*[78] and the *Oxford Dictionary of National Biography*[79].

Good luck with your research and enjoy your learning journey.

ENDNOTES

1   German philosopher, poet, cultural critic, philologist and
     composer whose work has exerted a profound influence on
     contemporary philosophy. He began his career as a classical
     philologist before turning to philosophy.

     Born: 15 October 1844, Röcken, Saxony, Prussia, German
     Confederation

     Died: 25 August 1900, Weimar, Saxe-Weimar-Eisenach, German
     Empire

     Recommended book(s):
     The Birth of Tragedy — Out of the Spirit of Music. Penguin Press
     (1993). First Published 1872.

     Beyond Good and Evil: The Philosophy Classic. Capstone
     Classics (2019). First published 1886

2 An Ancient Greek philosopher and polymath. His writings
   cover a broad range of subjects including physics, biology,
   zoology, metaphysics, logic, ethics, aesthetics, poetry, drama,
   music, rhetoric, psychology, linguistics, economics, politics,
   meteorology, geology and government. At the age of seventeen
   he travelled to Athens and entered Plato's Academy, whose own
   teacher was Socrates.

   Born: 384 BC, Stagira, Chalcidian League.

   Died: 322 BC, Euboea, Macedonian Empire

   Recommended book(s):
   Hall, E *Aristotle's Way: How Ancient Wisdom Can Change Your
   Life* Bodley Head (2020).

   Branes J *The Cambridge Companion to Aristotle* Cambridge
   University Press. (1995).

3 The Falklands War was a ten-week undeclared war between
   Argentina and the United Kingdom in 1982 over two British
   dependent territories in the South Atlantic: the Falkland Islands
   and its territorial dependency South Georgia and the South
   Sandwich Islands.

   The conflict started on 2 April 1982 and ended on 14 June 1982.

   Recommended book(s) & website(s):

Ramsey, G *The Falklands War: Then and Now* After the Battle. (2009)

Norman & Jones. *The Falklands War—There and Back Again: The Story of Naval Party 8901* Pen & Sword Military (2018).

https://www.youtube.com/watch?v=Fb01W-4G-no accessed May 2023.

4   Lucius Annaeus Seneca the Younger, usually known as Seneca, was a Stoic philosopher of Ancient Rome, a statesman, dramatist and satirist from the post-Augustan age of Latin literature. Seneca was born in Córdoba and raised in Rome, where he was trained in public speaking and philosophy.

Born: 4 BC, Córdoba, Hispania Baetica (present-day Spain)

Died: AD 65, Rome, Italy

Recommended book(s):
Letters from a Stoic: Epistulae Morales Ad Lucilium Kindle. Penguin Classics. (2004) First published 1886.

Letters from a Stoic. Collins. (2020) First published 1886.

5   Roman Emperor from 161 to 180 AD and a Stoic philosopher. He was the last of the rulers known as the Five Good Emperors, and the last emperor of the Pax Romana, an age of relative peace, calm and stability for the Roman Empire lasting from 27 BC to 180 AD. He is commonly known as the 'Philosopher King'. His *Meditations* were first written AD 161 to 180.

Born: 26 April 121, Rome, Italy

Died: 17 March 180, Vindobona, Pannonia Superior or Sirmium, Pannonia Inferior

Recommended book(s):
Torode, S *The Meditations: An Emperor's Guide to Mastery* (Stoic Philosophy Book 2) Ancient Renewal (2017)

Aurelius et al *Meditations: Marcus Aurelius*. Penguin Classics. (2006) Cognitive Behavioural Therapy (CBT)

6   CBT is a psycho-social intervention that aims to reduce symptoms of various mental health conditions, primarily depression and anxiety disorders. CBT focuses on challenging and changing cognitive distortions and their associated behaviours to improve emotional regulation and develop personal coping strategies that target solving current problems.

Recommended book & website:

Sokol, L *The Comprehensive Clinician's Guide to Cognitive Behavioural Therapy*. PESI Publishing & Media (2019)

https://www.nhs.uk/mental-health/talking-therapies-medicine-treatments/talking-therapies-and-counselling/cognitive-behavioural-therapy-cbt/overview/ accessed May 2023

7   Viktor Emil Frankl was a Jewish Austrian psychiatrist who founded logotherapy, a school of psychotherapy that describes the search for life's meaning as the central human motivational force. He survived the Holocaust and used that experience to help people with their personal life journeys.

Born: 26 March 1905, Vienna, Austria-Hungary

Died: 2 September 1997, Vienna, Austria

Recommended book(s):
Frankl V. *Man's Search for Meaning: The classic tribute to hope from the Holocaust.* (2004) Rider.

8   Emanuel James Rohn, professionally known as Jim Rohn, was an American entrepreneur, author and motivational speaker. Influenced people such as the life coach Tony Robbins. His goal was to help people be the best they can be in whatever they do.

Born: 17 September 1930, Yakima, Washington, U.S.

Died: 5 December 2009, West Hills, California, U.S.

Recommended book(s):
Ultimate Jim Rohn Library (2017). Audible.

Rohn J. *7 Strategies for Wealth and Happiness: Power ideas from America's business philosopher*. Harmony/Rodale (1996)

9   Albert Einstein was a German-born theoretical physicist, widely acknowledged to be one of the greatest and most influential physicists of all time. Einstein is best known for developing the Theory of Relativity, but he also made important contributions to the development of the theory of quantum mechanics.

Born: 14 March 1879, Ulm, German Empire

Died: 18 April 1955, Princeton, New Jersey, United States

Recommended book(s):
Einstein A. *Relativity. The Special and the General Theory*. Words Power (2022)

Einstein A. *Ideas and Opinions*. Crown Publications. (1995)

10 Edward Lee Thorndike was an American psychologist who spent
    nearly his entire career at Teachers College, Columbia University.
    His work and passion were set around psychology and the
    learning process and this led to the creation the law of effect
    principle, technically known as operant conditioning within
    behaviourism. It is linked to receiving agency whereby the body
    responds to an external stimulus. It formed the basis of our
    understanding of how we educate people today. Tip: Look at
    the work of B F Skinner to whom the theory of instrumental
    conditioning is attributed. He explored the consequences from a
    response that will determine the probability of it being repeated.
    This chimes with my theory of the compounding effect of
    learning.

Born: 31 August 1874, Williamsburg, Massachusetts, United
States

Died: 9 August, 1949, Montrose, New York, United States

Recommended book(s):
Thorndike E. *The Human Nature Club: An Introduction to the
Study of Mental Life.* Legare Street Press. (2016)

Or any good psychology book

11 Charles Perrow was an emeritus professor of sociology at Yale
    University and visiting professor at Stanford University. He
    authored several books and many articles on organisations, and
    was primarily concerned with the impact of large organisations
    on society and how complex organisations normalised accidents
    through the compounding of behaviour and habits.

Born: 9 February 1925, United States

Died: 12 November 2019, United States

Recommended book(s):
Perrow C *Normal Accidents: Living with High-Risk
Technologies* Princeton Paperbacks (1999)

Perrow C. *Complex Organizations: A Critical Essay.* Princeton
University Press. (2015)

12 Scott Snook is currently the MBA Class of 1958 Senior Lecturer
    of Business Administration at the Harvard Business School.
    Professor Snook has shared his military leadership insights in
    formal executive education programmes at Harvard. Professor
    Snook's research and consulting activities have been in the
    areas of leadership, leader development, change management,
    organisational systems and failure and culture. Scott presented
    the theory of practical drift away from optimum operational
    performance.

Born: 6 August 1958, United States

Recommended book(s):
Snook S. *The Handbook for Teaching Leadership: Knowing, Doing and Being.* Sage Publications Inc. (2011*)*.

13 Jordan Brent Peterson is a Canadian psychologist, author and media commentator. His sometimes-controversial views on cultural and political issues lead him to be described as conservative and of a Stoic slant. Peterson has described himself as a classic British liberal and a traditionalist.

Born: 12 June 1962, Edmonton Alberta Canada

Recommended book(s):
Peterson J. *Beyond Order and 12 Rules for Life* (2-Book Set Collection). Allen Lane (2021)

14 On 14 June 2017, a high-rise fire broke out in the 24-storey Grenfell Tower block of flats in North Kensington, West London, and burned for 60 hours. 72 people died, two later in hospital, with more than 70 injured and 223 escaping. One of the worst UK modern disasters.

Recommended website(s):
https://www.bbc.co.uk/news/uk-40301289 accessed May 2023.

15 The Hillsborough disaster was a fatal human crush during a
football match at Hillsborough Stadium in Sheffield, South
Yorkshire, England, on 15 April 1989. It occurred during an FA
Cup semi-final between Liverpool and Nottingham Forest in
the two standing-only central pens in the Leppings Lane stand,
killing 97 Liverpool FC supporters.

Recommended website(s):
https://www.bbc.co.uk/news/uk-england-merseyside-47697569
accessed May 2023.

16 Steve Peters is an English psychiatrist who works in elite sport.
He is best known for his work with British Cycling. Steve
specialises in the functioning of the human mind. He helps
people to understand how their minds work, and then develops
skills to help them be the best they can be regarding individual
performance and quality of life.

Born: 5 July 1953, England.

Recommended book(s):
Peters S. *The Chimp Paradox: The Mind Management
Programme to Help You Achieve Success, Confidence and
Happiness*. Vermilion. (2012)

Peters S. *A Path Through the Jungle*. Mindfield Press. (2012)

17 Adolf Hitler was an Austrian-born German politician who rose
to power as the leader of the Nazi Party, becoming Chancellor
in 1933 and then taking the title of Führer und Reichskanzler in
1934. Hitler's rule is a prime example of how a society can be
manipulated by driving a conformity and obedience culture.

Born: 20 April 1889, Braunau am inn, Austria.

Died: 30 April 1945, Berlin, Germany

Recommended book(s):
Ullrich & Chase *Hitler: Downfall 1939 – 1945*. Alfred A Knopf
Inc. (2020)

18 Corporate Manslaughter and Corporate Homicide Act 2007
puts the responsibility for the offence of corporate manslaughter
on an organisation if its activities cause a death. An organisation
fails on its duty of care to its employees if it is ignorant of
legislation such as health and safety laws. Management is liable
to prosecution if it lets a known risk become an avoidable issue
that ends in the death of an employee.

Recommended website(s):
https://www.legislation.gov.uk/ukpga/2007/19/contents accessed
January 2023

19 Stephen Richards Covey was an American educator, author, businessman and speaker. His most popular book is, *The 7 Habits of Highly Effective People*. Covey set principles and values separately; seeing principles as external natural laws and values as internal behaviours. Covey deemed that values set the foundation for people's behaviour, whereas principles determined the consequences from that.

Born: 24 October 1932, Salt Lake City, Utah, United States.

Died: 16 July 2012 Idaho, United States.

Recommended book(s):
Covey S. *The 7 Habits of Highly Effective People*. Simon & Schuster UK. 30th Anniversary Edition. (2020)

Covey S. *The 8th Habit*. Simon & Schuster UK. (2006)

20 Tenzin Gyatso, who lived as a refugee in India, became the Dalai Lama in February 1940. Dalai Lama is a title given by the Tibetan people to the foremost spiritual leader of the Gelug or 'Yellow Hat' school of Tibetan Buddhism.

Born: 6 July 1935. Taktser, Tibet

Recommended book(s):
Lama, Cutter et al. *The Art of Happiness: A handbook for living*. Hodder Paperbacks. (1999)

21 Socrates was an ancient Greek philosopher whose way of life, character and thought exerted a profound influence on Western philosophy. Socrates was a controversial figure in his native Athens, and his teachings were not valued in his time. At age 70, he was brought to trial on a charge of impiety and sentenced to death by poisoning by a jury of his own people. Socrates himself wrote nothing; however, his teachings were set down by others, primarily Plato who portrayed Socrates' work as having high integrity and great foresight. His work resonates today as powerfully as it did then.

Born: 470 BC, Athens, Greece.

Died: 399 BC, Athens Greece

Recommended book(s):
Hughes, B *The Hemlock Cup: Socrates, Athens and the Search for the Good Life.* Vintage (2011)

22 Professor Grint spent ten years in industry before switching to an academic career. He has taught at Brunel University and Oxford University and held Chairs at Lancaster and Cranfield Universities. He is currently Professor of Public Leadership and Management at Warwick Business School, UK. His research looks at leadership in all its forms.

Unknown date of birth.

Recommended book(s):
Grint K *Fuzzy Management: Contemporary Ideas and Practices at Work*. Oxford University Press. (1998)

Grint K *Leadership: a very short introduction*. Oxford University Press. (2010)

23 Anthony Jay Robbins is an American author, coach, inspirational speaker and philanthropist. Tony Robbins is known for his coaching seminars, self-help books and online courses. He was influenced by the work of Jim Rohn.

Born: 29 February 1960. Los Angeles, California, United States.

Recommended book(s):
Robbins A *Unlimited Power: The New Science of Personal Achievement*. Simon & Schuster Inc. (2001)

24 Abraham Harold Maslow was an American psychologist who created Maslow's hierarchy of needs, a theory of psychological health predicated on fulfilling innate human needs in priority, culminating in self-actualization. Maslow was a psychology professor at Brandeis University, Brooklyn College, New School for Social Research, and Columbia University.

Born: 1 April 1908. New York., United States.

Died: 8 June 1970. California, United States.

Recommended book(s) and website(s):

Maslow A *Motivation and Personality* Harper & Brothers. 2nd Edition TBS Publications. (1987) First Published (1954)

Maslow A. *Hierarchy of Needs: A Theory of Human Motivation.* Wilder Publications. (2022) First Published (1954)

Or any good general psychology book.

25 Frederick Irving Herzberg was an American psychologist who became one of the most influential names in business management. He is most famous for introducing the Motivator–Hygiene theory. His 1968 publication *One More Time, How Do You Motivate Employees?* had sold 1.2 million copies by 1987 and was the most requested article from the Harvard Business Review.

Born: 18 April 1923. Lynn, Massachusetts, United States.

Died: 19 January 2000. Salt Lake City, Utah, United States.

Recommended books

Herzberg F *One More Time, How Do You Motivate Employees?* Harvard Business Review Press. (2008) First Published (1968)

Or any good organisational psychology book.

26 Prader-Willi Syndrome is a rare genetic condition that causes a wide range of physical symptoms, learning disabilities and behavioural challenges. It is usually noticed shortly after birth. Prader-Willi Syndrome is caused by some missing genetic material in a group of genes on chromosome number 15. This leads to a number of problems and is thought to affect part of the brain called the hypothalamus, which produces hormones and regulates growth and appetite. Typical features of Prader-Willi Syndrome are delayed growth and persistent hunger.

Recommended website(s):
https://www.pwsa.co.uk accessed July 2023.

27 International Standards Organisation (ISO) standards are internationally agreed by experts across the world. They are a framework and process that help organisations to perform effectively and safely. The standards are formed from the wisdom of people with expertise in their subjects and who know the needs of the organisations they represent: manufacturers, sellers, buyers, customers, trade associations, users and regulators. Their standards are set around a series of belts and are focussed on the reduction of waste across all areas of a business.

Recommended website(s):
https://www.iso.org/home.html accessed June 2023.

28 Six Sigma is a set of techniques and tools for process improvement. It was introduced by American engineer Bill Smith while working at Motorola in 1986. Six Sigma strategies seek to improve manufacturing quality by identifying and removing the causes of defects and minimising variability in manufacturing and business processes. Closely linked to Demings PDCA cycle and the development of Total Quality Management.

Recommended website(s):
https://www.sixsigmacouncil.org/six-sigma-definition/ accessed June 2023.

29 Bruce Lee was a Hong Kongese/American martial artist, actor and philosopher. He was the founder of Jeet Kune Do, a hybrid martial arts philosophy drawing from different combat disciplines that is often credited with paving the way for modern mixed martial arts. Bruce wrote *Tao of Jeet Kune Do* following a serious back injury which led to his philosophical teachings.

Born: 27 November 1940. San Francisco, California, United States.

Died: 20 July 1973. Kowloon, Hong Kong

Recommended book(s):
Lee B. *Tao of Jeet Kune Do*. Bodo (2009)

30 Jonathan Peter Wilkinson CBE is an English former rugby union player. A fly-half, he played for Newcastle Falcons and Toulon and represented England and the British and Irish Lions. He is particularly known for scoring the winning drop goal in the 2003 Rugby World Cup Final and is widely acknowledged as one of the best rugby union players of all time.

Born: 25 May 1979. Frimley, England.

Recommended website(s):
https://www.bbc.co.uk/sport/av/rugby-union/25018784 accessed June 2023.

31 A pioneer in performance psychology, his passion is for his pursuit of continual improvement and revolutionising the performance abilities of sports and business people alike. Dr Alred has influenced many sports and business peak performers as an elite performance coach.

Recommended book and website(s):
Alred D *The Pressure Principle: Handle Stress, Harness Energy, and Perform When it Counts* Penguin Life (2017)

https://davealred.com accessed June 2023.

32 Daniel Goleman is an author, psychologist and science journalist. For 12 years, he wrote for The New York Times, reporting on the brain and behavioural sciences. His 1995 book *Emotional Intelligence* was on The New York Times Best Seller list for a year and a half, a bestseller in many countries, and is in print worldwide in 40 languages.

Born: 7 March 1946. Stockton, United States.

Recommended book and website(s):
Goleman D *Emotional Intelligence. 25th Anniversary Edition.* Bloomsbury Publishing. (2020)

https://www.danielgoleman.info accessed June 2023.

33 Steven Paul Jobs was an American business magnate, industrial designer, media proprietor and investor. He was the co-founder, chairman and CEO of Apple; the chairman and majority shareholder of Pixar; a member of The Walt Disney Company's board of directors following its acquisition of Pixar; and the founder, chairman and CEO of NeXT.

Born: 24 February California, United States.

Died: 5 October 2011. California, United States

Recommended book(s):
Isaacson, W *Steve Jobs: The Exclusive Biography*. Little Brown (2011)

34 Elon Reeve Musk is a business magnate and investor. He is the founder, CEO and chief engineer of SpaceX; angel investor, CEO and product architect of Tesla, Inc.; owner and CTO of Twitter; founder of the Boring Company; co-founder of Neuralink and Open AI; and president of the philanthropic Musk Foundation.

Born: 28 June 1971, Pretoria, Transvaal, South Africa

Recommended book(s):
Isaacson, W *Elon Musk*. Simon & Schuster Inc. (2023)

35 Wayne Douglas Gretzky is a Canadian former professional ice hockey player and former head coach. He played 20 seasons in the National Hockey League for four teams from 1979 to 1999.

Born: 26 January 1961. Ontario, Canada.

Recommended book(s):
Gretzky W. 99 *Stories of the Game* G P Putman's Sons. (1900)

Gretzky & Reilly *Gretzky: An autobiography* Harpercollins. (1990)

36 Jürgen Norbert Klopp is a German professional football manager and former player. Jurgen Klopp currently mangers Liverpool Football club. who is the manager of Premier League club Liverpool. Regarded by many as one of the best managers in the world.

Born: 16 June 1967. Stuttgart Germany.

Recommended book(s):
Neveling N. *Jurgen Klopp*. Ebury Press (2020)

37 Sir Alexander Chapman Ferguson is a Scottish former football manager and player, best known for managing Manchester United from 1986 to 2013. Regarded by many as one of the greatest managers of all time and has won more trophies than any other manager in the history of football.

Born: 31 December 1941. Glasgow Scotland.

Recommended book(s):
Ferguson A. *Alex Ferguson My Autobiography*. Hodder Publications (2014)

38 David Hawkins was a professor whose interests included the philosophy of science, mathematics, economics, childhood science education and ethics. He was also an administrative assistant at the Manhattan Project's Los Alamos Laboratory and later one of its official historians.

Born: 28 February 1913. El Paso, Texas, United States.

Died: 24 February 2002. Boulder, Colorado. United States.

Recommended book(s):
Hawkins D. *Power versus Force: The hidden determinates of human behaviour*. Hay House. (2012)

39 Wilfred Emmanuel-Jones is a British businessman, farmer and founder of The Black Farmer range of food products. He argues that our natural instinct for caution is one of the greatest barriers to making progress in life and shows how embracing jeopardy is essential if you want to succeed and go further in life by learning to escape the fears that stop us from achieving our ambitions.

Born: 7 November 1957. Clarendon, Jamaica.

Recommended book(s):
Emmanuel-Jones W. *Jeopardy: The Danger of Playing It Safe on the Path to Success* Piatkus. (2018)

40 John Winston Ono Lennon was an English singer, songwriter, musician and peace activist who achieved worldwide fame as founder, co-songwriter, co-lead vocalist and rhythm guitarist of The Beatles. Lennon's work was characterised by the rebellious nature and acerbic wit of his music, writing and drawings, on film and in interviews.

Born: 9 October 1940 Liverpool, England.

Died: 8 December 1980 New York City, United States.

Recommended book and website(s):
Norman P. *John Lennon: The Life.* Harper (2009)

https://www.britannica.com/biography/John-Lennon accessed June 2023.

41 Charles Robert Darwin was an English naturalist, geologist and biologist, widely known for his contributions to evolutionary biology. His proposition that all species of life have descended from a common ancestor is now generally accepted and considered a fundamental concept in science.

Born: 12 February 1809. Shrewsbury, England.

Died: 19 April 1882. Down, Kent, England.

Recommended book and website(s):
Darwin C. *On the Origin of Species*. Macmillan Collectors Library (2017) (First published 1859)

https://www.britannica.com/biography/Charles-Darwin accessed June 2023.

42 Basil Reynolds, visionary coach, author, inspirational speaker, personal development specialist. 'Personal development that encourages well-being.' Former Hip Hop artist with London Rhyme Syndicate.

Born: 26 December 1966. London, England.

Recommended book(s):
Reynolds B. *Finding Your Music Inside: Your inner algorithm to more meaningful life*. Freeworld Speech. (2020)

43 The 1979 Three Mile Island accident was a partial meltdown of
the Three Mile Island Unit 2 reactor on the Susquehanna River
in Londonderry Township, Pennsylvania, United States. It began
at 4 a.m. on 28 March 1979 and released radioactive gases and
radioactive iodine into the environment. Although no one died in
the incident, scientific studies have linked it to cancer cases that
cropped up in the years following the accident.

Recommended website(s):
https://www.britannica.com/event/Three-Mile-Island-accident
accessed June 2023

44 The 1985 Bradford City football stadium fire occurred during a
Football League Third Division match on Saturday 11 May 1985
at the Valley Parade stadium in Bradford, West Yorkshire,
England, killing 56 spectators and injuring at least 265. The
stadium was known for its antiquated design and facilities,
which included the wooden roof of the main stand.

Recommended website(s):
https://www.bbc.co.uk/sport/football/32388297 accessed June
2023

45 The 1987 Kings Cross London Tube disaster fire caused 31 fatalities, including one of our own (fire service) Colin J. Townsley G.M., Station Officer. A fire under a wooden escalator suddenly spread into the underground ticket hall in a flashover. The fire began at approximately 7:30pm on 18 November 1987 at King's Cross St Pancras tube station, a major interchange on the London Underground.

Recommended website(s):
https://www.london-fire.gov.uk/museum/history-and-stories/historical-fires-and-incidents/the-kings-cross-fire-1987/ accessed June 2023

46 John Lydon, aka Johnny Rotten, has claimed that he was banned from the BBC after speaking out against Jimmy Savile. On Piers Morgan's *Life Stories*, the Sex Pistols front man said that during a 1978 interview he claimed Savile was 'into all sorts of seediness. We all know about it but we're not allowed to talk about it. I know some rumours.' Jimmy Savile was a television icon who used his positions to carry out an alarming level of sexual abuse.

Recommended website(s):
https://www.youtube.com/watch?v=_fO-f6UJw04https://www.theguardian.com/music/2015/sep/24/john-lydon-says-he-was-banned-from-bbc-over-jimmy-savile-comments accessed June 2023

47 James Wilson Vincent Savile was an English DJ and television and radio personality who hosted BBC shows including *Top of the Pops* and *Jim'll Fix It*. During his lifetime, he was well known in the United Kingdom for his eccentric image and his charitable work. However, he abused his position. It is now known that Jimmy Savile sexually abused hundreds of children and women at the height of his fame.

Investigators believe he preyed on around 500 vulnerable victims as young as two years old at institutions including the BBC's broadcasting studios, 14 hospitals and 20 children's hospitals across England.

Recommended website(s):
https://www.theguardian.com/media/2014/jun/26/jimmy-savile-sexual-abuse-timeline accessed June 2023

48 The Bible is a collection of religious texts or scriptures that are held to be sacred in Christianity, Judaism, Samaritanism and many other religions.

The Bible – Luke 23:34 'Father, forgive them, for they do not know what they are doing.'

49 In 2000, the BBC broadcast an hour-long documentary called *Five Steps to Tyranny* narrated by Sheena McDonald. It looks at how ordinary people can do monstrous things in the presence of authority. The documentary covers the work of a variety of people including Professor Philip Zimbardo and Stanley Milgram and looks at how horrific things happen in the world across five easy steps. We would like to believe only evil people carry out atrocities. But tyrannies are created by ordinary people, like you and me.

Recommended website(s):
https://www.youtube.com/watch?v=PeBisBQblFM accessed June 2023

50 Stanley Milgram was an American social psychologist, best known for his controversial experiments on obedience conducted in the 1960s during his professorship at Yale University. Milgram was influenced by the events of the Holocaust, especially the trial of Adolf Eichmann, in developing the experiment.

Born: 15 August 1933. Bronx, New York, United States.

Died: 30 December 1984. Manhattan, New York, United States.

Recommended website(s):
https://psychology.fas.harvard.edu/people/stanley-milgram accessed June 2023

51 Philip George Zimbardo is an American psychologist and a professor emeritus at Stanford University. He became known for his 1971 Stanford Prison experiment, which was later severely criticised for both ethical and scientific reasons. However, his work resonates around the world today.

Born: 23 March 1933. New York City, United States.

Recommended website(s):
https://www.zimbardo.com accessed June 2023

52 Solomon Eliot Asch was a Polish-American Gestalt psychologist and pioneer in social psychology. He created seminal pieces of work on impression formation, prestige suggestion, conformity and many other topics. His line experiment is a clear insight into conformity and obedience.

Born: 14 September 1907. Warsaw, Poland

Died: 20 February 1996. Haverford, Pennsylvania, United States.

Recommended website(s):
https://www.youtube.com/watch?v=TYIh4MkcfJA accessed June 2023

53 Jane Elliott is an American diversity educator. As a schoolteacher, she became known for her 'blue eyes/brown eyes' exercise, which she first conducted with her third-grade class on 5 April 1968, the day after the assassination of Martin Luther King Jr. The publication of compositions which the children had written about the experience in the local newspaper led to much broader media interest in it.

Born: 30 November 1933, Ricevilla, Iowa, United States

Recommended website(s):
https://www.youtube.com/watch?v=dLAi78hluFc accessed June 2023

https://janeelliott.com Accessed August 2023

54 Martin Luther King Jr. was an American Baptist minister and activist who was one of the most prominent leaders in the civil rights movement from 1955 until his assassination in 1968. His famous speech was 'I have a dream' on 28 August 1963. Five years later in 1968 he was assassinated in Washington on a freedom march.

Born: 15 January 1929, Atlanta, United States

Died: 4 April 1968. Memphis, United States.

Recommended website(s):
https://www.youtube.com/watch?v=o8dzxh7Ybqw accessed June 2023

55 OFSTED: The Office for Standards in Education, Children's Services and Skills is a non-ministerial department of His Majesty's Government, reporting to Parliament. Ofsted is responsible for inspecting a range of educational institutions, including state schools and some independent schools, in England.

Recommended website(s):
https://www.gov.uk/government/organisations/ofsted accessed June 2023

56 William Edwards Deming was an American engineer, statistician, professor, author, lecturer and management consultant. Deming's PDCA cycle from his work during the 1950s sets the foundation for most standards today.

Born: 14 October 1900. Sioux City, Iowa, United States.

Died: 20 December 1993. Washington D.C. United States.

Recommended book and website(s):
Deming W.E. *Out of Crisis.* MIT Center for Advanced Engineering Study (1986)

Or any good psychology or quality standards book

https://deming.org/deming-the-man/ accessed June 2023

57 The JIT inventory system is a management strategy that aligns raw-material orders from suppliers directly with production schedules. Companies employ this inventory strategy to increase efficiency and decrease waste by receiving goods only as they need them for the production process, which reduces inventory costs. This method requires producers to forecast demand accurately.

Recommended website(s):

https://www.accountingformanagement.org/just-in-time/ accessed June 2023

58 The Royal Navy gymnastic display team that travelled around mainland UK and Europe performing the mast-manning and window ladder displays. I was part of that team in 1983 and button boy on four occasions.

Recommended website(s):

https://www.youtube.com/watch?v=3zLdQbNRiWA accessed May2023

https://www.youtube.com/watch?v=2JvhlzSijCw accessed May2023

59 Royal Navy Field Gun Crew competition is a contest between teams from various Royal Navy commands, in which sailors compete to transport a field gun and its equipment over and through a series of obstacles in the shortest time. The competition evolved during the early years of the 20th century. The 'Command' format, negotiating walls and a chasm, was held annually at the Royal Tournament in London from 1907 until 1999, apart from the periods during the World Wars. Now disbanded, it was once considered one of the world's toughest and most dangerous sports.

Recommended book and website(s):
https://www.youtube.com/watch?v=Rxz4aPoudv8 accessed May2023

60 The Second Manchester Bombing occured in the evening of 22 May 2017 in the Manchester Arena, attendees, mainly young people, had just enjoyed a concert by Ariana Grande. While they were making their way through the Arena's large foyer towards the exits, where many parents were waiting to collect their children, Salman Abedi, who entered the foyer as the concert was ending, detonated a bomb contained in a rucksack he was wearing killing 22, with 139 physically injured and many more suffering psychological injuries. The inquiry that followed was highly critical of all emergency services regarding safety measures that allowed the incident to happen in the first place and that affected their subsequent response.

Recommended website(s):
https://www.bbc.co.uk/news/uk-england-manchester-53824562 accessed May2023

https://www.bbc.co.uk/news/uk-england-manchester-57499326 accessed May2023

61 The government is suing accountancy firm KPMG for £1.3bn over its audit of construction giant Carillion, which collapsed into administration in 2018. Carillion had run up debts of more than £7bn when it went bust.

Recommended website(s):
https://www.bbc.co.uk/news/business-60243464 accessed May2023

62 Raymond Meredith Belbin is a British researcher and management consultant best known for his work on management teams. He is a visiting professor and Honorary Fellow of Henley Management College in Oxfordshire, England. His Belbin exercise is used to define key roles in the work environment. Belbin and Tuckman are theories that complement each other.

Born: 4 June 1926. Sevenoaks, Kent, England.

Recommended book and website(s):
Belbin & Brown *Team Roles at Work*. Routledge. (2022)

Or any good organisational psychology book

https://www.belbin.com/about/dr-meredith-belbin accessed May2023

https://www.belbin.com/about/why-use-belbin accessed May2023

63 Bruce Wayne Tuckman was an American psychological researcher who carried out his research into the theory of group dynamics. In 1965, he published a theory known as 'Tuckman's stages of group development'. According to this theory, there are five phases of group development: Forming, Storming, Norming, Performing and Adjourning.

Born: 24 November 1938. New York, United States.

Recommended book and website(s):

Tuckman et al. *Learning and Motivation Strategies: Your Guide to Success* Pearson (2007)

Or any good organisational psychology book

https://www.belbin.com/resources/articles-directory/belbin-and-tuckman accessed May2023

64 Samuel Langhorne Clemens, known by his pen name Mark Twain, was an American writer, humourist, entrepreneur, publisher and lecturer. He was praised as the greatest humourist the United States has produced. His quotes resonate with a lot of life situations today.

Born: 30 November 1835. Florida, United States

Died: 21 April 1910. Connecticut, United States.

Recommended book and website(s):

Hardy, S. *Mark Twain Quotes of Wit and Wisdom: Inspirational Quotes from America's Greatest Humorist to Make You Smile, Think and Grow!* Independently Published (2021)

https://www.britannica.com/biography/Mark-Twain accessed May2023

65 Confucius was a Chinese philosopher and politician of the Spring and Autumn period who is traditionally considered the paragon of Chinese sages. Confucius's teachings and philosophy underpin East Asian culture and society, remaining influential across China and East Asia to this day.

Born: 551 BCE. Zou State of Lu, China.

Died: 479 BCE. St. River, State of Lu. China

Recommended book and website(s):
Confucius *Analects: With Selections from Traditional Commentaries* Grapevine India (2022)

Beaulac, A. *Sitting with Lao-Tzu: Discovering the Power of the Timeless, the Silent and the Invisible in a Clamorous Modern World*. Apocryphile Press (2017)

https://www.cief.org.cn/kzxy/ accessed May2023

66 Plato was an ancient Greek philosopher born in Athens during the Classical period. In Athens, Plato founded the Academy, a philosophical school where he taught the philosophical doctrines that would later become known as Platonism. Plato was a student of Socrates and the teacher of Aristotle. Plato was one of the most famous, respected and influential philosophers of all time. He recognised that society was driven by a social structure of a governing class, warriors and workers. He thought the human soul contained reason, spirit and appetite. Plato's *Dialogues of Socrates* stand the test of time.

Born: 428 BC, Athens, Greece.

Died: 348 BC, Athens Greece

Recommended book(s):
Translated by Gill, C *The Symposium*. Penguin Classics. (2003)

67 Glaucon was the older brother of Plato, and like his brother was amongst the inner circle of Socrates' young students. He is primarily known as a major conversant with Socrates in *The Republic* by Plato, in which they discussed the Parable of the Cave.

Born: 445 BC. Collytus.

Died: 424 BC. Megara

Recommended book(s):
Howland J. *Glaucon's Fate, Myth and Character in Plato's Republic.* Paul Dry Books (2018)

68 The Rwandan genocide occurred between 7 April and 15 July 1994 during the Rwandan Civil War. During this period of around 100 days, members of the Tutsi minority ethnic group, as well as some moderate Hutu and Twa, were killed by armed Hutu militias. The most widely accepted scholarly estimates are around 500,000 to 662,000 Tutsi deaths. It is a prime example of the *Five Steps to Tyranny* and its horrific potential outcome.

Recommended website(s):
https://www.bbc.co.uk/news/world-africa-26875506 accessed May2023

https://www.britannica.com/event/Rwanda-genocide-of-1994 accessed May2023

69 Glastonbury Music and Arts Festival is a five-day festival of contemporary performing arts that takes place in Pilton, Somerset, England. In addition to contemporary music, the festival hosts dance, comedy, theatre, circus, cabaret and other arts. It is my spiritual home.

Recommended website(s):
https://www.glastonburyfestivals.co.uk accessed June 2023

70 Monty Python's *The Meaning of Life* is a 1983 British musical comedy film written and performed by the Monty Python team, directed by Terry Jones. *The Meaning of Life* was the last feature film to star all six Python members before the death of Graham Chapman in 1989.

Recommended website(s):
Find it on most video steaming platforms.

71 Portia Nelson was an author, singer, composer, lyricist, painter, photographer and actress. She appeared in such films as *The Sound of Music*, *Dr Dolittle*, *The Trouble with Angels*, and *The Other*, and she starred in the television soap opera *All My Children* as the nanny Mrs Gurney for many years. Nelson wrote, directed, and performed a musical based on 'There's a Hole in My Sidewalk'. In addition, she wrote music and lyrics for revues, television specials, films and songs.

Born: 27 May 1920. Brigham City, Utah. United States.

Died: 6 March 2001. New York City, United States.

Recommended book(s):
Nelson P. *There's a Hole in My Sidewalk: The Romance of Self-Discovery.* Atria Paperbacks. (2018)

72 John Howard Jones is a British musician, singer and songwriter. He had ten top 40 hit singles in the UK between 1983 and 1986; six of which reached the top ten, including 'What Is Love?' and 'Things Can Only Get Better'. Howard kindly allowed me to use his lyrics from 'New Song'.

Born: 23 February 1955. Southampton, England.

Recommended website(s):
https://www.youtube.com/watch?v=9fjg7N_mGaU accessed May 2023

https://www.youtube.com/watch?v=XPaZKHsiZ4A accessed May 2023

http://howardjones.com accessed May2023

73 The inspirational poem, 'Children Learn What They Live' was written by Dorothy Law Nolte in 1955. Wrote parenting newspaper articles in her twenties and thirties. The author of over 40 poems, mostly unpublished.

Dorothy was still going strong in her late 70s when she wrote and published two books, translated into twenty plus languages. More books followed, primarily in Japan, where she was greatly admired. Her family has created this website to share this wisdom with new generations of parents.

Born: 12 January 1924. Los Angeles, California, United States.

Died: 6 November 2005. United States.

Recommended website(s):
https://childrenlearnwhattheylive.com accessed May 2023

74 Epictetus was a Greek Stoic philosopher. He was born into
slavery at Hierapolis, Phrygia and lived in Rome until his
banishment, when he went to Nicopolis in north-western Greece
for the rest of his life. His teachings were written down and
published by his pupil Arrian in his *Discourses* and *Enchiridion*.

Born: Ad 50. Hierapolis, Phrygia (Now Turkey).

Died: Ad 135, Nicopolis (Now Greece)

Recommended website(s):
https://plato.stanford.edu/entries/epictetus/ accessed May 2023

https://www.britannica.com/biography/Epictetus-Greek-
philosopher accessed May 2023

75 My mate Budgie served with me on HMS Invincible for two and
half years. He tragically died the day after the Falklands War
cease fire. He has been an inspiration for my life and this book.

Born: 7 December 1962. Rawtenstall, Lancashire, England.

Died: 16 June 1982. Falkland Islands.

Recommended website(s):
https://falklands35blog.wordpress.com/2021/06/20/falklands-35-brian-marsden/ accessed May 2023

76 HMS Invincible was the Royal Navy's lead ship of her class of three light aircraft carriers. She was launched on 3 May 1977 as the seventh ship to carry the name. She was originally designated as an anti-submarine warfare carrier but was used as an aircraft carrier during the Falklands War.

Recommended website(s):
https://www.youtube.com/watch?v=gvKFAbKoCHY accessed May2023

https://www.seaforces.org/marint/Royal-Navy/Aircraft-Carrier/R-05-HMS-Invincible.htm accessed May 2023

https://www.hmsinvincible82.co.uk accessed June 2023

77 Sub-Officer Paul Metcalf died as he tried to save a student from the lake in Holcombe Brook in Bury, Greater Manchester, in September 1999. He was a dedicated 25-years-served fire officer and hero who served in Greater Manchester fire and rescues service.

Born: 1959. Manchester England. Died: 5 September 1999. Holcombe Brook, Bury, England.

Recommended website(s):

http://psdiver.com/images/1999_UK_FIREFIGHTER_PSD_Paul_
Metcalfe_-ROPE-Secure.pdf accessed June 2023

78   Hornblower S. *Oxford Classic Dictionary OUP* Press (2012)

79   Oxford Dictionary of National Biography. https://www.
oxforddnb.com accessed August 2023.

ABOUT THE AUTHOR

DAVE ARMSTRONG is proud to be born and brought up in Liverpool. He was blessed with loving parents who gave him a solid and happy start in life. He is a mix of Scottish and Irish heritage. His grandad, a veteran of both First and Second World Wars, through many stories and coaching sessions, grounded Dave in values and principles that would stay with him throughout his life.

Joining the Royal Navy Fleet Air Arm in 1979, as a 17-year-old, consolidated Dave's values and principled foundation. Here he was taught about self-responsibility, controlling your mind, being positive, the importance of always seeking to learn and the power of working as a team: principles that were to form the core of his book *7 Rules to a Good Life*. Dave served on HMS Invincible aircraft carrier as a crash firefighter, one of the most dangerous work environments there is with fighter jets and helicopters landing and launching only metres away.

He saw active service during the Falklands War in 1982 with 847 Helicopter Commando Squadron, serving as part of the land force. He witnessed the rawness and madness of war and death, losing his close friend Budgie and discovering the body of a very young Argentinian soldier. These events had a profound effect on him.

Towards the close of his five-year military career, Dave joined the Royal Navy Display Team and performed high-risk aerial displays, including 'button boy' standing on the top of a 97-foot mast, performing to thousands.

Due to the mental trauma of war, Dave left the military and joined the British fire service, serving 27 years before retirement in 2013. Some of Dave's proudest moments were working with and leading teams on shouts in the centre of Manchester, from road traffic accidents, house and building fires, to major incidents. His skilled leadership was spotted by his mentor Mick Bitcon who brought him into headquarters to design training and command systems.

However, it was the totally avoidable Hillsborough Football disaster that killed 97 Liverpool supporters and the death of a colleague Paul Metcalfe at a water incident that ignited his fascination for why humans seem to avoid the warnings of initial risk, before they do something about it.

In 2000, he earned the unique opportunity to lecture and direct courses at the National Fire Service Officers' College where he served for four years. This is where his love of coaching people to be the best they can be grew. In 2004, he returned to his home brigade to lead on research and design structures for their modernisation project. The brigade at the time had been deemed 'poor' by national auditors. This project concluded in 2005 when the fire brigade reversed its fortunes and achieved a mark of 'very good'. Dave then took a temporary post as station commander of the Eccles area. However, the findings of the modernisation report showed the brigade had a lot of work to do strategically, which didn't rest well with many, and Dave began to be bullied by senior managers. The bullying concluded with him losing everything and ending up sleep rough on Euston station in 2007. This profound low moment changed Dave for ever. He began to rebuild his life and the *7 Rules to a Good Life* grew.

Around this time, he was offered a parallel career working for universities and colleges, designing courses and lecturing in leadership, organisational behaviour, group dynamics and project management. These days, his focus is on coaching, writing and authorship.

In recent years Dave has faced some personal challenges, losing his mum to covid in 2020 and his wife Nicky in 2017 to cancer. On each occasion Dave found the power to 'go again' using his 7 rules to live his life to the best he can with respect to those who have passed, celebrating their lives rather than mourning their deaths.

Now in his early 60s, Dave has at last found his good life in his work to help as many people as he can to discover and create their own good life via his Live Life Smarter programme and his book *7 Rules to a Good Life*.

Printed in Great Britain
by Amazon